HERTFORDSHIRE RAMBLES

HERTFORDSHIRE RAMBLES

Fourteen Country Walks
around Hertfordshire

Liz Moynihan

With Historical Notes

COUNTRYSIDE BOOKS
NEWBURY, BERKSHIRE

First Published 1988
©Liz Moynihan 1988, 1994
Updated and reprinted 1990, 1991
This new edition published 1994

COUNTRYSIDE BOOKS
3 Catherine Road
Newbury, Berkshire

ISBN 1 85306 293 6

To Barney the hipless wonderdog who happily walked with me
for over 250 miles in the research of this book

Cover photograph taken by Alan Charles
Sketch maps by Sarah Talks

Produced through MRM Associates Ltd., Reading
Typeset by The Midlands Book Typesetting Company
Printed and bound in England by J. W. Arrowsmith Ltd, Bristol

Contents

8 •
Ashwell

9
• Newsells

7 •
Hexton

10 •
Buntingford

6 •
St Pauls Walden

11 •
Benington

5 •
Knebworth

12 •
Much Hadham

4 •
Ayot St Lawrence

3 •
Aldbury

13 •
Hertingfordbury

14 •
Essendon

1 •
St Albans

N

2 •
Sarratt

Sketch map showing the locations of the walks.

Introduction

The walks in this book have been chosen because they encompass all the elements of the Hertfordshire countryside: chalk escarpments, river valleys, wooded parkland, rolling grain fields, as well as villages, a market town and the outskirts of a city.

Hertfordshire has a vast web of footpaths created over the centuries and a wealth of historical interest from its long established past and its many important country estates. These factors make it ideal for rambling. It is easy to get right off the beaten track. The rewards of tackling the various parts of the county lie in unexpected views and discoveries.

All the walks are circular and their starting points have space for car parking. For those who like to break their walk for refreshment the names of good pubs and places serving tea along or near the routes are mentioned.

The historical notes are designed to provide basic information about the places of interest along the route, and will be found at the end of each chapter.

The sketch map that accompanies each walk is designed to guide walkers to the starting point and give a simple yet accurate idea of the route to be taken. The walks are all along public footpaths or permissive paths. Some paths are waymarked (blue or yellow arrows on posts), some are signposted, but always there are the clear instructions to point the way. For those who like the benefit of detailed maps the relevant Ordnance Survey 1:25000 Landranger series will be useful. Please remember the Country Code and make sure gates are not left open or any farm animals disturbed.

No special equipment is needed to enjoy the countryside on foot, but do wear a stout pair of shoes and remember that at least one muddy patch is likely even on the sunniest day.

INTRODUCTION

Many hours of enjoyment have gone into preparing these walks. I hope that the reader will go out and enjoy them too.

Liz Moynihan
May 1994

3/1/95.

St Albans, Verulamium and Gorhambury

Introduction: The old streets and dominating cathedral on the outskirts of St Albans lead the walker down among the Roman ruins in the valley of the river Ver, and on into the park and farmlands of the ancient estate of Gorhambury, just off Roman Watling Street. All the elements of this walk are bound together by historic ties which criss-cross each century of history. The Gorhambury estate road is not a public right of way, but Lord Verulam kindly allows access to walkers. Please respect this and keep on the main drive only. A specially designated walk – the Ver-Colne Valley Walk passes along the first section of the drive. There are lots of interesting places to visit (see historical notes) so allow plenty of extra time.

Distance: About 6 miles. Time taken about 2½ hours (excluding visits). There is a SHORT CUT for those wishing to do only part of the route. Map – Landranger 166, Luton, Hertford (GR 137077).

Refreshments: Waffles in Kingsbury Water Mill. Light meals, coffee, teas (licensed). There are several pubs offering meals and bar snacks in St Albans, including *The Fighting Cocks, The Six Bells, The Rose and Crown, Lower Red Lion, Black Lion* and the *Blue Anchor*.

How to get there: From the A1(M) at Hatfield follow signs to St Albans (A414, A1081). Follow the road into the centre of St Albans (there are signs to Verulamium). In the city centre go over the main crossroads (Peahen pub on the left) then instead of following the main A5183 (Redbourn) road which bears round to the right, carry on straight ahead down George Street, Romeland Hill (cathedral on left) and then

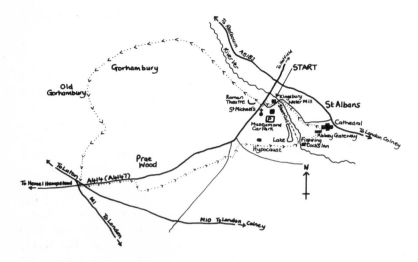

down Fishpool Street. At the bottom of the hill, opposite
Kingsbury Water Mill, turn left for a short distance. Lay-by
parking is available just over the bridge from the Mill,
or right next to the Mill in Prae Close. Further on near
Verulamium Museum, there is a Pay and Display car park.

The walk: Cross the bridge over the river Ver turning right
out of Kingsbury Water Mill. Walk down St Michael's
Street which is full of interesting old houses and two pubs.
Some way along cross the road to Darrowfield House (the
old Dower House of Gorhambury) and bear left to visit
Verulamium Museum and St Michael's Church opposite.
Walk through the churchyard to the main road (A4147
formerly A414). Cross bearing slightly to the right and turn
left down Gorhambury Drive (the route of Roman Watling
Street). On the left is the Roman theatre.

The gated estate road leads through pleasant fields
studded with woodlands, and is lined with an interesting
variety of trees of different ages. The river, hidden in a dip
over the field to the right flows into ancient fishponds further
on. Ignore the signs to the Ver walk on the right and carry
on along the road past late 17th century Maynes Farmhouse
(with Victorian front) on the right. A roadway goes off to the
left opposite the farm, but the walk continues straight ahead
along the main drive, past a white gatehouse further on on

the right. Eventually the drive forks; left is the private drive to Gorhambury mansion, and the route follows the estate road curving to the right round the back of the mansion to the ruins of Old Gorhambury rising romantically on the right. The ruins, and the Palladian-style mid 18th century Temple Cottages to the left further on, provide interesting views. The drive then bends left downhill past cattle sheds and then right to Stud Cottage. Just beyond go through a gate, then straight on past a right turn to Westwick Hall, until, further ahead beyond Hill End Farm and the pretty timbered cottage opposite, the drive comes out under an M10 road bridge.

Turn left out of Beechtree Lane along the verge of the busy A4147 (formerly A414) under another road bridge. Walk for about half a mile alongside a hedgerow and then a wood on the left. Just before a gateway into the wood cross the road and turn right into a field along a footpath signposted to St Albans past a pretty pond on the left. Walk along the line of trees towards the corner of a wood ahead. From here the footpath should go diagonally across the field to meet the far corner of the wood, but if crops make this difficult to follow, go right and then left along the edge of the wood. Leave the corner of the wood and follow a farm track ahead. The track bears off to the right but follow the footpath that goes ahead across the field following a straggly line of trees, roughly parallel to the main road further over the field on the left. At the last tree make for a small wood ahead, passing through a fence and over a second field to a signpost at a road. Cross the road (Bedmond Lane), turn to the left a short way, and then go right at a footpath signpost through wooded wasteland and onto an estate road (Mayne Avenue).

Carry on left down the road, across a grass strip and onto King Harry Lane. Cross and go through a five-barred gate opposite to Verulamium Park with a wonderful view of the cathedral on the hillside ahead. Strike out diagonally across the park to the right between woods to the right and the Roman Hypocaust to the left protected by the small brick building erected over it. Beyond are lakes and lumps of Roman wall. Make for the edge of woods in the distance just behind the railings guarding the ruins of the Roman city's south-east gateway. Turn left here along a metalled track (The Causeway), past the end of the lakes to the Fighting Cocks Inn by a bridge over the river Ver opposite the 18th century Abbey mill.

(The walk can be shortened here by turning left by the lakes and walking along the river bank back to St Michael's Street and Kingsbury Water Mill.)

For a brief look at part of the old town, walk up Abbey Mill Lane from the Fighting Cocks past pretty houses and cottages to the Abbey Gateway and the Cathedral and Abbey Church of St Albans on the right. Through the Gateway bear left past the small Romeland Garden (an area which commemorates the burning of Protestant martyrs, and continue down Romeland Hill into Fishpool Street and its lovely houses of varying ages. The Lower Red Lion pub is on the right and 17th century St Michael's Manor, now a hotel, further down on the left. At the bottom of the hill are the Black Lion and the Blue Anchor just where the street comes out opposite the lump of Hertfordshire puddingstone standing outside Kingsbury Water Mill.

Historical Notes

Kingsbury Water Mill: A Georgian brick facade hides Elizabethan timbers in this pretty mill restored to working order by the Gorhambury Estate. The mill, on the site of a mill mentioned in the Domesday Book, has belonged to the Gorhambury Estate since the 16th century at least, and ground the grain grown there until the late 1920s. It is open at weekends in winter, and every day except Mondays in summer.

Verulamium Museum: A must for archaeologists and historians, the museum contains a wealth of Roman and Iron Age finds, excavated by Sir Mortimer Wheeler among others, and wonderful mosaics. Open daily.

St Michael's Church: Built on the site of the Roman forum by a Saxon abbot, this ancient church has Roman tiles built into its flint walls. Inside is a magnificent marble effigy of Sir Francis Bacon, Lord Keeper of the Great Seal, who died in 1626 and was buried at his own request in this church because it was, as he said, 'the only Christian

Church within the walls of Old Verulam'. Open in the afternoons only.

Roman Theatre: The only one in Britain that can be seen in its entirety. Like others in France it is associated with a temple (not visible) nearby. Originally built between AD 125–150 on the Greek model and seating 1,500 people, it underwent various changes over the years, before falling into disrepair and eventually becoming a rubbish tip. Now restored, it is open daily from 10 am to 5 pm.

Gorhambury House: Built in 1777–84 (architect Sir Robert Taylor) for the third Viscount Grimston in the Palladian style, the present house was refaced in Portland stone in 1956. It houses Britain's longest chronological collection of family portraits (from 1446 to the present day) and memorabilia of Sir Francis Bacon among other treasures. It is open on Thursdays from May to September 2–5 pm.

Old Gorhambury: The porch and part of the hall are all that remain of the Tudor courtyard house begun in 1563 by Sir Nicholas Bacon, Francis' father. Sir Nicholas, Lord Keeper of the Great Seal to Queen Elizabeth I, had two sons. The eldest, Anthony, died in 1601, and Francis inherited and then altered the house. He rose to great power under James I, but in 1621 was found guilty of corruption. Following his release from the Tower after four days, he devoted his life to letters and learning. He loved Gorhambury and made a famous garden there.

Verulamium Park: Originally part of the Gorhambury estate (the manor had once belonged to St Albans Abbey), the park with its extensive Roman remains was sold to the town in the 1930s. The lakes were dug in 1929 and 1935. Just round the corner from the museum is Grebe House (a 16th century half-timbered building, moved from Watford and re-erected in 1982 for the Herts and Middlesex Wildlife Trust. The shop and information centre are open daily except in January and February.

The first Verulamium was pre-Roman – reputedly the headquarters of the Catuvellauni tribe. After their defeat the first Roman city was begun by the river in AD 43.

It was attacked and fired by Boudicca in AD 61. A new Verulamium was built by AD 79 on a larger scale and this developed into an important city over the next hundred years.

Fighting Cocks Inn: This interesting octagonal timber-framed building, probably part of the old wall which surrounded the medieval abbey, was once a pigeon house and then became an inn in 1600. Cock fights were held there for many years.

Abbey Gateway: Dating from about 1365 and once the principal entrance to the monastery, this old building is now part of St Alban's School. It was used as the town gaol after the Dissolution until 1868.

The Cathedral and Abbey Church of St Alban: This great building stands on the spot where Albanus, a Roman soldier, was executed in AD 209 for protecting a priest who had converted him to Christianity. He was the first British martyr. The Abbey was probably founded by Offa, King of Mercia, in the 8th century, and was a Benedictine Abbey until the Reformation. It is the oldest surviving monastic church in western Europe. The building standing today dates mainly from Norman times. The huge tower was built from Roman brick from nearby Verulamium. The nave is the longest in Europe. Its many other treasures can be appreciated with the help of a detailed guide book (obtainable from the Cathedral Bookstall).

WALK TWO

Sarratt

Introduction: The little river Chess forms the border between Hertfordshire and Buckinghamshire in the south-west of the county, and the villages which climb the slopes of the valley here have a special prettiness. This walk explores the beauties of one of them, Sarratt, with its long hummocky village green with a duckpond at one end and a strange-looking village pump in the middle. The walk crosses meadows to reach Sarratt Church End, now a hamlet consisting of a few dwellings, a row of Gothic almshouses and a lovely 12th century church. The walk continues through a patchwork of woods, well-hedged lanes and pastoral fields full of cows.

Distance: About 5 miles with a possible SHORT CUT. Time taken 2–2¼ hours. Suitable only for the reasonably active as the route crosses at least a dozen stiles. Map – OS Landranger 166 Luton, Hertford (GR 041996).

How to get there: Sarratt is off the A41 between Watford and Hemel Hempstead. Turn onto the B4505 on the outskirts of Hemel Hempstead and follow the signs through Bovingdon, then on to Chipperfield and then Sarratt. Park on the slip road next to the village green.

Refreshments: The *Boot* or the *Cricketers* at Sarratt both serve food.

The walk: Walk in a southerly direction passing the Boot pub (peg-tiled and white-painted) and the yellow and red-brick Baptist chapel on the left and a selection of shops on the right. Beyond the duckpond near the end of the green is the Cricketers pub. Pass the post office and its neighbouring house, the Old Forge, on the right. Next to the Old Forge a footpath is signposted to Church End.

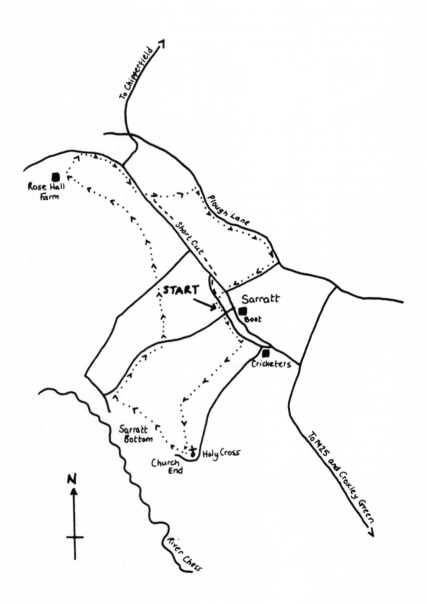

Turn right along this past cottages. Go over a metal stile into a small meadow and carry straight on keeping to the left-hand side. Cross another metal stile next to a gate and carry on. Cross a third metal stile to the left of a gate and again go ahead. Climb a fourth stile by gates onto a green ride. Go across this and over a wooden stile (plastic arrow marker) and follow the path through woods bordering gardens on the left. Come out onto a lane. Cross and take the kissing gate and stile slightly to the left. This leads into a large meadow. Walk in a diagonal line rightish up the field towards the pointed roof of the Church of the Holy Cross. Go over a stile and through a kissing gate into the churchyard. It is well worth exploring this fascinating church in its rural setting some way from the village. The Old Rectory is next door and opposite are some pretty Gothic 19th century almshouses.

At the church gate there is a footpath sign to Sarratt Bottom. Retrace your steps through the churchyard and back through the kissing gate and over the stile into the meadow again. This time, keep to the left boundary and follow the line of trees on the left. Towards the end of the field is a three-barred opening. Climb this into the next meadow and keep on the same line as before, this time with the hedgerow on the right. At the corner of the field bear left and carry on to about halfway along the hedgerow where another three-barred opening leads to the right through the hedge. Climb this and follow the hedgerow on the left down the field, go through a kissing gate on the boundary and down some steps onto a tiny lane. A detour can be made to the river down the lane on the left.

However, the main walk turns right up this pretty lane hedged with hazel and bracken. As the lane begins to go up through woods there is a public footpath signpost on the left. Turn along this. Very soon there is a marker post with the bridleway signed with a white arrow along the main path ahead and the footpath arrowed in yellow to the left. Follow the smaller footpath to the left. It curves to the right near huge old oak trees. At a junction of paths bear leftish. The path comes to a main track leading to a wooden gate with a stile marked with a yellow marker to the right of it. Turn left and go over the stile and walk along between a wood on the right and a row of cupressus trees on the left. Cross another stile and go straight ahead across an open field. Go through a gap in a fence and continue rightish down the hedgerow on the right towards more fencing in the corner. There is a house over on the field on the right. Cross another stile onto a little lane, cross it and climb another stile by a public footpath sign into a meadow. Go in a diagonal line slightly to the right across it. As you go up the gentle slope make for the wooden gates which come into view. Another big house stands over on the right. Cross the stile to the right of a wooden five-barred gate (yellow arrow marker). This leads onto a broad farm track. Cross over this and go over the stile on the other side. A notice says 'Private Land Keep to Footpath'. Go diagonally slightly to the right across this field towards a fence with a stile across the field. Cross the stile into the next field and go straight across this keeping a barbed wire fence on the left. Climb bars to the left of a metal gate, turn left down the lane and keep on past a notice saying 'Private Road Caution'. This leads to 17th century Rose Hall Farm. The track has an open field on the left with woods in the distance and a wood on the right for part of its length.

Carry straight on at a grassy triangle, then before reaching the farmhouse turn right at a barn down another broad farm track. There is a white arrow marker on the fence. Walk past a large farm barn on the left. There is an open field on the right and a hedge on the left. Come out onto a little lane by a footpath signpost pointing back to Church End. Turn right along this pretty lane hedged mainly with holly studded with lovely mature oaks. The land slopes sharply down on the left. The lane comes out onto a bigger road; turn right here to Sarratt.

For the SHORT CUT continue along the main road back to the village. To continue the walk, pass the main entrance to Rose Hall Farm on the right and shortly after this look for a footpath signpost on the left by a small metal railing. Two footpaths are signposted through the woods. Take the right-hand path which follows white-painted arrows on the trees and skirts through the edge of the woodland with a field beyond on the right. The wood is studded with dells and dips. Cross a stile onto a lane and turn right.

This is Plough Lane and is like a tunnel, with trees meeting overhead. Ignore footpaths signposted off the lane and carry on along it. Pass a flint and weatherboarded cottage and Dellfield House on the left by an area of grass. Ignore the footpaths which go off here to Commonwood Common and keep on along the lane to a small crossroads. Turn right here up Red Lion Lane signposted to Sarratt. This small hedged lane climbs steeply up to the houses of Sarratt. Cross the main road and turn left along the green to the parking place.

Historical Notes

Sarratt Green: This long and hummocky village green full of old pits (perhaps dried up ponds) and wild flowers still has one flourishing duckpond and an old pump (looking like a giant knife cleaner). The names of the converted houses which surround it recall the former businesses of the village – the bakehouses, forge, saddlery and wheelwrights. The green was probably a watering place for sheep along an old drovers' route and two pubs remain of at least five that existed only a few decades ago. The Boot dates back to 1739.

Church End, Sarratt: Standing near the manor house is a pretty row of 16th century almshouses (some of the earliest in the country). They were rebuilt by Ralph Day of Sarratt Hall in 1821 and incorporate pretty Gothic windows, an old Sun Insurance plaque and a Victorian post box set in the wall. The main part of Sarratt was once here but many houses disappeared as more people took up residence round the green. In the 17th century, the Cock Inn was the mortuary for plague victims, who were buried in the adjoining field. The inn is said to have a specially wide door through which the coffins were brought.

Holy Cross church: This small 12th century church (near a Roman site) is built in the shape of a cross, using mainly flint and Totternhoe stone with some Roman red brick and chunks of Hertfordshire pudding stone in strategic positions. The saddleback tower is unique in Hertfordshire. Inside are Norman arches, a panelled sanctuary, 700-year-old wall paintings and an alabaster monument to William Kingsley who died in 1611. The carved pulpit and tester are early 17th century. Restoration was carried out in 1864 by Sir George Gilbert Scott, who seems to have had a hand in most of the restorations of churches for miles around, though he actually worshipped at Holy Cross, Sarratt.

Aldbury and Ashridge

Introduction: Aldbury, one of the prettiest villages in Hertfordshire, is the starting point for this walk on the south-western side of this county in the Chiltern hills. Graceful old houses and cottages back on to the steep, thickly wooded slopes of the Ashridge Estate, now under the ownership of the National Trust. The walk climbs uphill into the woods and then passes through them for a mile or so, eventually coming out into farmland which drops sharply to the Grand Union Canal below. After a short stroll along the towpath past locks and canal cottages, the rambler climbs gently uphill again through more farmland and woods, then meanders back downhill to the other side of Aldbury, along village streets, and thence to the village green and pond.

Distance: About 8 miles. Time taken 3½–4 hours at a leisurely pace. There is a SHORT CUT which will almost halve the distance, for those whose time is limited. Map – Landranger 165 Aylesbury (GR 965125).

Refreshments: The *Greyhound* and the *Valiant Trooper* in Aldbury (bar food). Snacks at the National Trust tearoom near the Bridgewater Monument. The *Cow Roast* across the canal from Cow Roast lock (pub food).

How to get there: Aldbury is near Berkhamstead just off the Hemel Hempstead to Aylesbury (A41) road. Go through Berkhamstead towards Aylesbury, and just on the outskirts of the town at Northchurch, turn right onto the B4506 (Ashridge) road. After about 2½ miles, turn left at a signpost saying Aldbury and Tring, in the middle of the woods. Follow the road for a mile or so round a hairpin bend and down into the village of Aldbury. Parking is marked out near the village green outside the Greyhound pub.

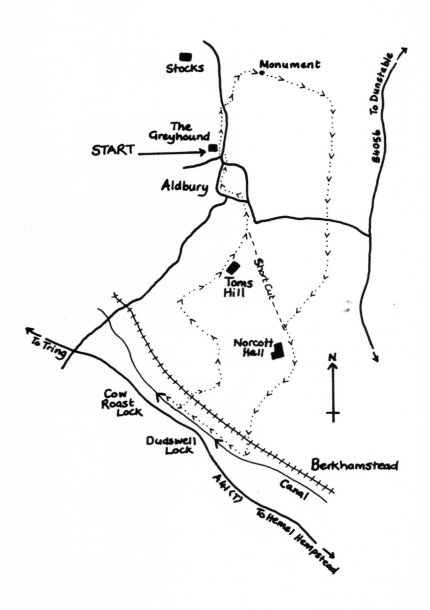

The walk: Turn left out of the pub away from the village pond. Walk down the road past attractive houses and cottages. At the end of Aldbury village, a public footpath points to the right beside a house. Ignore this and walk further on down the road. Before reaching a collection of buildings by the road (Stocks Farm) a signpost on the right points up a few steps, over a stile, and up the hedgerow on the left. Halfway up the hedgerow cross a stile to the left into a field. Walk across the middle of this, roughly parallel with the road towards a cottage and house ahead. An imposing house called Stocks, now a hotel, together with its old farmhouse, timbered barns and stabling down by the road, can be seen over on the left. The woods of Ashridge rise steeply on the right hand side. Cross a stile and turn right up a drive past an elegant red brick house on the left. Go up a steep little slope to a gate. Walk straight on uphill. Keep on the main path which narrows a little before long. A house can be seen on the left with a clearing next to it. After a rough circle of beech trees, the path veers very slightly to the right and comes out through the trees at a clearing with a tall column in the middle of it (the Bridgewater Monument). A little further on, on the right, is the National Trust Information Centre and tearoom next to a white cottage.

Carry on straight ahead away from the Monument down a wide grassy avenue with a road through the middle. About a mile and a half away, at the end of the avenue, can be seen a glimpse of Ashridge House (now a Management College). About a quarter of the way down this avenue, there is a concreted dead end at right angles to the road. Turn down this and go over a tree trunk barrier onto a ride through the woods. The path is well trodden through the trees; follow it straight ahead. It carries on for some distance crossing several cross tracks. The track eventually reaches a fenced off area of wood on the left. Pass it keeping straight on. On the left is a field reclaimed from the surrounding woodland.

Go over yet another major cross track (there are lots of tiny paths off to the left and right which should be ignored). This one is marked by a concrete post and the back of a footpath notice. Carry on past a murky looking pond on the left, down by the side of a lodge and onto a road. Cross the road and follow the path (signposted) straight ahead again down a green ride by a conifer wood (Rail's Copse) planted in 1967. The ground is very muddy because of the close tree cover and reaches quite a boggy area.

When the conifer copse ends the track emerges into mixed woodland by a yellow arrow on a low post. Follow its direction straight ahead (the path may not be very obvious and may deviate round fallen trees). Ignore all other tracks at this point.

After two or three hundred yards near the edge of the wood with open land beyond, the path meets a bridleway running across it at a slight angle along two lines of very old beeches. Turn right along the bridleway (which runs from the road near the turn to Aldbury right through to Norcott Hall Farm). The double line of beeches carries on with occasional gaps like missing teeth, amidst fallen or truncated branches, occasional saplings, and sometimes some rather weedy holly. Eventually the track narrows into a more scrubby, brackeny area, past a large dell on the right with dead trees all round.

Through the trees on the right can be seen a field. Follow a track bearing a little to the right and keep on ahead for some distance through the trees on a path which is roughly parallel with the field to be seen nearby on the right. This eventually comes out on to a green near a white farm gate on the right. There is a good farm track leading to it.

(For a SHORT CUT turn right here and cross the stile by the gate. Follow the right hand hedge keeping it to the right. At the end of a field cross a stile into another field through a kissing gate and over another stile. Carry straight on keeping fence and hedgerow to the left this time. Soon can be seen the pleasant facade of Tom's Hill House over the field on the left. Shortly after this, a stile takes the walker into woods. The path leads ahead through the woods to meet the drive to Tom's Hill House. Turn right down the drive to the Aldbury Road. Here follow instructions for the longer version of the walk to return to Aldbury.)

To continue the main walk, turn left down the track which becomes a gravelled and then a metalled drive, past cottages on the right, then the stables and the smart pineapple-topped entrance gates to Norcott Hall. The drive bears round to the right (really now a road). Follow the road downhill quite a long way, ignoring the fork to Norcott Court on the right. Eventually the road rises slightly to a bridge over the railway.

Shortly after this the canal bridge comes into sight. Turn right along the edge of the canal on the towpath near a cottage called Lockside. Walk past a second lock (Dudswell) and continue on past another lock keeper's cottage. At the third lock (Cow Roast) go under the bridge, up steps and turn right back on yourself to the bridge. Then turn left down the roadway past a waterworks building and the gates to Cow Roast Marina on the left. Follow the road right round, then not far along is a footpath sign on the left. Go through the hedge here, over a stile, across a small field to a foot-bridge over the railway. Once over the bridge, cross another small field to a line of young trees by a track. Turn right onto this track and follow along a wire fence bearing left at the corner towards Norcott Court Farm. Turn left round the end of the garden onto a track which leads to the farmyard. Bear right to a big gate and stile near a hay barn on the left. Go diagonally left across the field towards a large tree and wood beyond. Towards the corner, ignore the gate in the boundary on the right and aim for the gate in the corner, next to which is a stile. Cross the stile and go ahead over the field keeping a knot of beech trees to the right.

The field opens out to the right and left, but go across the middle, aiming for the corner of a hedgerow which borders a bumpy field beyond. At the hedgerow corner, keep straight on along the hedge (a lovely mixed one), keeping it to the right, to the next corner. Here a path goes through the hedge slightly to the right and passes up a strip of woodland to a stile in a fence. Cross this and go diagonally over the field to the left, over the brow of a hill to woodland ahead. The field slopes steeply down on one side and rises to woodland on the right, giving good views over the countryside below. Make for the corner of the field diagonally opposite. The path goes straight out of this field, over a stile and down into another one with a wire fence on the right.

Follow a hedgerow and spinney downhill keeping them on the right. Just before the corner of the spinney, go through a five barred gate to the right into the spinney.

Carry on ahead up the path through the trees. The wood falls steeply away to fields on the left and rises sharply on the right. The path climbs, passing remains of a gateway and goes on to a metal gate. Go through and straight ahead along the track through small fields through more metal gates. Go past barns on the right, through another large farm gate past a red brick half timbered cottage on the left and the buildings behind Tom's Hill on the right. Follow the road past a house and cottage on the left and a triangle of grass outlined in stones on the right through woodland to the bend on the road to Aldbury, and the meeting point with the SHORT CUT route.

A little further on down the main road to the left a signposted path leads left down a steep wooded slope to the outskirts of Aldbury. The track comes out at a seat at the top of a back lane. Follow on down the lane between houses, bear right at the bottom and follow the road past the *Valiant Trooper* and back to the pond on Aldbury Green.

Historical Notes

Aldbury: Some of the prettiest and most interesting houses and cottages of this fairly large village border the triangular village green with its pond and old stocks and whipping post at one end.

Stocks: This gracious renovated 18th century house, almost hidden by trees, is now a smart hotel and country club. Nearer the road are the beautiful old Tudor house and barns of Stocks Farm; in the farmyard is a chequered brick dovecote dated 1753. Stocks was owned in the 19th century by Mrs Humphrey Ward (1851–1920), a well-known novelist of the period. She was one of the first lady magistrates, despite being resolutely against women's suffrage. She was related to the brilliant and the famous, being the granddaughter of Dr Arnold of Rugby fame, the mother-in-law of historian G. M. Trevelyan, and aunt of Aldous and Julian Huxley.

Ashridge Estate: Ashridge has existed as an estate for more than 700 years. In the 13th century, Edmund, son of Richard of Cornwall and grandson of King John, was the first recorded owner and founded a religious house here run by Augustinian monks from France. This survived until the Reformation. The deer park had been used for hunting for centuries. In 1926, the National Trust acquired a large part of the Ashridge Estate, and over the years more land has been purchased adding up at the present time to about four thousand acres of downland, commonland, woodland and farmland stretching from Ivinghoe Beacon to Berkhamstead.

Detailed information can be obtained from the National Trust Information Centre and Shop (open afternoons only in season) situated near the Monument where there is also parking.

Bridgewater Monument: Erected in 1832 by Wyattville in memory of the third Duke of Bridgewater (1736–1803) who lived at Ashridge, this Doric column is one hundred feet high and has 172 steps to the top. It is open in the afternoons in season for twenty pence. The Duke was called 'the Father of Inland Navigation' because of his record as a pioneer of Britain's canal system.

Ashridge House: Ashridge began as a monastery in the 13th century, passing briefly after the Reformation into the ownership of Elizabeth I who spent some time there as a young girl. Eventually it was bought by the Egerton family (later Earls and Dukes of Bridgewater). By the end of the 18th century, the Canal Duke had allowed the property to fall into disrepair and his cousin who inherited Ashridge commissioned James Wyatt to rebuild it in 1808, thus creating the spectacular neo-Gothic mansion existing today. The house, now a Management College, does not belong to the National Trust and is not open to the public, but the gardens can be visited on Saturday and Sunday afternoons in season. Humphrey Repton designed much of the present garden, though it is said that Capability Brown had made an earlier contribution.

The Grand Union Canal: Beginning life as the Grand Junction Canal, the Grand Union became a system of at least eight separate canals making up an important transport system for southern England. It was built mainly in the late 18th and early 19th centuries and is a major engineering feat, climbing up the edges of the Chilterns. At Cow Roast the summit level is reached at about 400 feet above sea level. Associated canal architecture of bridges, locks and cottages is interesting, and at Cow Roast the old Toll Office still exists.

Ayot St Lawrence

Introduction: This walk ranges from the tranquil water meadows of the river Lea, near territory shrouded in ancient history, to the cosy fields and woods of Ayot St Lawrence, tucked away off the beaten track at the centre of a web of tiny lanes. Close by Waterend and the river Lea is another Roman road, and Devil's Dyke. Ayot St Lawrence is famous in more recent history as the home and work place of George Bernard Shaw. In between these two diverse spots, the walk passes close to a number of notable houses and a wealth of pastoral scenery: altogether a most enjoyable few hours.

Distance: 7 miles. Time taken about 2½–3 hours at a leisurely pace. Map – OS Landranger 166 Luton, Hertford (GR 203139).

Refreshments: The *Brocket Arms* in Ayot St Lawrence. This attractive pub serves excellent food, cream teas on summer Sundays, and also offers accommodation.

How to get there: Leave the A1(M) at Junction 4 signposted to Hertford (A414), Hatfield (A1001) and Welwyn Garden City (A6129). Follow the signs to Welwyn Garden City (A6129) then to Wheathampstead (B653). After about two miles a small right turn leads to Waterend and Ayot Green. Park carefully on the road near the ford.

The walk: On either side of the ford are two interesting houses: medieval White Cottage and lovely old Waterend House. Opposite Waterend House by a flint wall follow a broad track with a swan sign denoting the Lea Valley Walk. Carry straight on past the end of the wall, by the water meadows of the river Lea on the left seen through a scrappy hedge. When the bridleway bears right, continue ahead

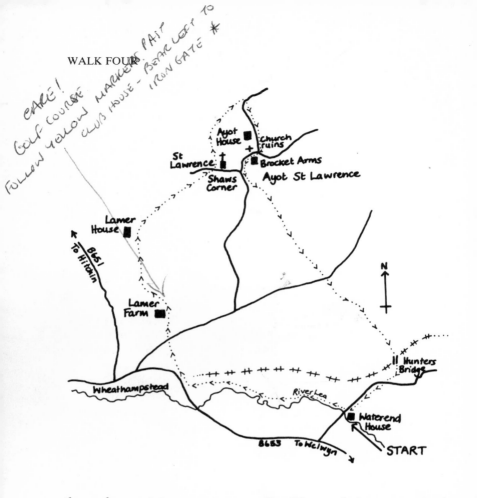

through a gateway next to a stile. The path is waymarked and still carries the Swan sign.

Follow a hedge on the left and walk ahead through a field. Go into a second field with the path somewhat down in a dip, then cross one more stile (still with the sign of the Swan) into a meadow. Walk through the middle of this meadow with the river meandering through on the left, and then bear right up the hill at a pylon near the end of the meadow. Go over a stile by a gate. A public footpath is signposted to left and right. Turn left along it to a gate, then right along a bridleway going uphill.

At the track of an old railway going to left and right, turn left, then right fairly soon, up a bank and over a stile. Carry on straight ahead along a good track with woodland on the right and a hedge on the left. Come out over a stile onto a little road. Cross over and go through posts by a metal gate and up a track immediately opposite. Continue along this track into Lamer Park. The track bears left to Lamer Farm, but the footpath goes on straight ahead up a grassy path for a short distance. Turn left into the field and follow a line of trees across to a wood. The trees are marked with white arrows. Bear right along the edge of the woods, and after going through a high metal gate at a T junction of tracks, turn right away from a white house, through woods and fields to left and right. Then follow a metalled drive towards a neatly kept hedge surrounding Lamer House on the left. Apsley Cherry Garrard who took part in Scott's last Antarctic Expedition lived here.

Bear right at a T junction, then arriving at a second junction, take a right hand track over a stile down a lovely lime avenue marching through fields dotted with trees and copses. On the right can be seen the imposing red-brick facade of Bride Hall, a listed late 16th century manor house, set down in a dip. At a gate halfway down the avenue, negotiate another stile and carry straight on. Reaching the end of the avenue, ignore the track into woodland on the right and go ahead down a track which is signposted 'Public Footpath to Ayot St Lawrence'. The track skirts through woodland (thick with bluebells in spring) with glimpses of houses on the right. Cross a stile by a gate and turn right along the road. After a house called Arnoldsfield take a left footpath signposted to St Lawrence's Church and follow the driveway to the church.

Go through the gate on the right and round to the front of the church. The scroll shaped epitaph to Mary Ann South is just in front of the portico. Go through a pretty iron gate at the other side of the church and over a stile into a field beyond. Skirt round the edge of the field keeping the trees on the left. A stile soon appears on the left, but avoid it and keep on round the field towards a large conifer. The footpath should cut the corner here towards another large conifer and a stile beyond. Go over the stile and along the edge of a field (keeping the hedge on the right) towards a large converted barn ahead. At the drive to Abbotshay, the lovely old house beyond the barn on the left, turn right down the drive. Continue on, past fields sprinkled with mature trees to the old brick garden wall of the Manor House further on. Continue straight on past the front of the house, and out through metal gates. On the right is the drive leading to Ayot House. Continue on down the left hand fork of the drive towards a gatehouse by the road.

Turn right along the main road towards the Brocket Arms pub and the timbered cottages of Ayot St Lawrence. On the other side of the road is the ruined church. Just past the original Ayot Rectory on the corner, the road bears left to a junction where Shaw's Corner stands. Follow the road straight on downhill ignoring the right turn past the house, turn left round the corner by the old home of Shaw's great friends, the Winstens, and left off the main road onto a bridleway.

This bridleway goes for some distance along the edge of fields and woodlands, then opens onto a large field on the right. Keep along the edge of the field again for some way, then turn left through a small gap in the boundary fence into woodland. This is a permissive route running parallel to the bridleway through Stocking Springs Wood, a Herts and Middx Wildlife Trust Nature Reserve. A stile at the end of the path gives onto a road past a gateway. Cross the road slightly to the left and follow the bridleway along a well-defined route with a fence on the right and a wood on the left. The path bears slightly to the left, and then goes into a field on the right. Go through the gate and continue ahead along the edge of woodland by a field. The bridleway follows on round the woodland, then goes left past some conifers. There is a triangular-shaped clearing on the right.

Keep the conifers on the left and continue on between two fenced off patches of trees, down a small hill, and continue round the woodland keeping it on the left. Bear left through a gap in the hedge and then right keeping the hedge on the right, and an arable field on the left. Just before the old railway bridge (Hunter's Bridge) turn right and climb up onto the track of the old railway (part of the Ayot Greenway). Walk along it to the right. Fairly soon there is a waymarked sign to the left up steps and out into an open field.

Turn right along trees on the right and come out onto the road. Turn right along the road and walk past red-brick cottages on the right down a narrow lane bordered with holly and mixed hedging back to Waterend House where the walk began.

Historical Notes

Waterend House: This beautiful mellow Jacobean (1610) brick house, wreathed in wisteria, with its stone mullions and multiple chimneys, is said to be the birthplace of Sarah Jennings, later Duchess of Marlborough. One of its magnificent barns was transported to and rebuilt in the centre of St Albans and is now a restaurant called Waterend Barn.

St Lawrence's Church: This unusual church was built in 1778 in Grecian revival style by Nicholas Revett for the squire Sir Lionel Lyde. It was said to be modelled on the temple of Apollo at Delos. The altar is at the west end instead of the usual east end. The church is made of brick and painted stucco with Portland stone dressings. Sir Lionel and his wife are buried in separate pavilions on either side of the portico. The churchyard contains an epigraph to seventy year old Mary Ann South – 'her time was short'.

The ruins of the old church (mainly 14th century with some earlier features) stand just off the village street, dominating the scene with its partly battlemented early 15th century tower. The church was being taken down on the orders of Sir Lionel Lyde because it spoiled the view from his new mansion, Ayot House, but demolition was stopped by the Bishop of Lincoln in whose diocese the parish then was. There are still some interesting monuments inside.

Ayot House: This handsome square mid 18th century house was built by Sir Lionel Lyde to replace the old Manor House. During the Second World War it was lived in by ex-King Michael of Romania. It then became a famous silk farm with royal connections. It is now divided into several flats.

The Manor House: This mellow brick house, remodelled in the late 17th century from the original 16th century timber framed building was the original Manor House, once owned by Sir Richard Parr, whose daughter Catherine became Henry VIII's last queen.

Tudor buildings: Opposite the old church in the main street of Ayot St Lawrence are various much altered but mainly Tudor cottages. The name of the Brocket Arms (part 14th century but much restored in the 17th century) refers to the Lord of the Manor, Lord Brocket of nearby Brocket Hall. The old post office next door, still with its post box let into the wall, was the scene of Shaw's one act play *A Village Wooing*. On the corner is the Old Rectory, built about 1790 with an earlier core. It was the subject of *Ayot Rectory* by Carola Oman who lived at nearby Bride Hall. There is a memorial to her and her husband in the church. Her dates are 1897–1978.

Shaw's Corner: This rather severe late Victorian house, built about 1902 as the New Rectory, was the home of George Bernard Shaw for 44 years until his death in 1950. He renamed it *Shaw's Corner*. The house is full of his books and possessions and feels uncannily as if he has just left it to go for a walk. In the garden is the simple summerhouse where he did much of his work free from interruption. When he died his ashes were scattered in the garden. It is now owned by the National Trust and is open Sunday to Thursday afternoons in season (for details telephone Stevenage 820307).

Knebworth Park and Graffridge Wood

Introduction: The combination of ancient deer park, mixed woodland, open fields, magical mansion and village houses of varying ages and styles makes this central Hertfordshire walk a particularly fascinating one. Knebworth is designated a Country Park, and though it contains various amusements, and is used for occasional pop festivals, rallies and sporting events, this walk avoids the most frequented areas and ventures outside the confines of the park through fields and woods. Extra time can be taken to visit Knebworth House during the summer months when it is open. The walk is not suitable for dogs as it is difficult to lift them over the high deer fences. Deer and sheep may be seen in the park.

Distance: 4¼ miles plus an optional ¼ mile to view the lake. Time taken about 1½–2 hours. Map – OS Landranger 166 Luton, Hertford (GR 230203).

Refreshments: The *Lytton Arms* at the start and finish of the walk serves pub food. The *Barns Restaurant* in the park serves meals in season.

How to get there: Knebworth lies about 28 miles north of London. Leave the A1(M) at Junction 7 (Stevenage South A602) ignoring the signs to Knebworth House. Continue along the A602 to a second and then third roundabout. Turn right here onto the B197 following the signs to Knebworth. In the centre of the town take a right turn signposted to Old Knebworth and follow this road to Old Knebworth past the station, bearing left some distance further on at a junction opposite the park. Park carefully near the *Lytton Arms* further down the road on the left.

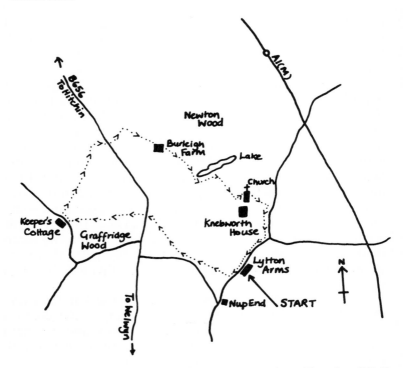

The walk: Some of this walk is part of a Circular Walk route and is mostly waymarked. Turning left out of the pub, cross the road and walk along the pavement past the Lytton almshouses as far as Park Gate House nearly opposite Slip Lane. The footpath goes to the right through the yard. Go over a stile with holly hedges to the right, then bear right through a small patch of woodland, go through a barrier then left and up a high step stile over the deer fence into Knebworth Park. Follow the path straight ahead keeping the fence and cottage beyond on the left, past the Monument on the right. Cross another high stile, sparing a glance for the Gothic gatehouse through the trees on the left, and keeping a fence on the left, walk down towards a small stream below late 17th century Wintergreen Cottages gleaming white up ahead. Bear left over a third high stile and through a small strip of woodland keeping the cottages to the right.

Cross the B656 (Hitchin Road) and enter Graffridge Wood along the signposted path opposite. Stay on the wide path which bears right along the edge of the wood first, then bears to the left. Ignore all other tracks. The path becomes a wide ride between conifers and crosses over a bisecting ride until it spills out onto a small lane.

Turn right along the lane, passing Keeper's Cottage, until opposite the next cottage, a signposted right turn to Langley through a gap in the hedge leads across a field, towards a little knot of oak trees. Go through a gap in the hedge by the trees, and follow the hedge slightly to the right which leads onto a wood bounded by a ditch. Follow on along the field edge keeping this to the right, then over a stile by a metal gate into another field. Make for the stile in the wire fence opposite. Cross this, passing a small pond and some marshy indentations and scrub, and then bear right towards a gate and stile in the corner of the field. Climb the steep bank and cross the B656. To reach the footpath, there are some rough steps down the bank on the other side beside a signpost.

Follow the path along by a wood on the left. Halfway along turn right (waymarked) across a large field up to a gate and stile beside a small wood. Cross another field straight ahead to a stile by Burleigh Farm (a listed 17th century timber-framed building) and barns.

Go straight ahead through the farmyard, through two gateways, then cross a field to a third gate/stile or use the signposted permissive footpath to the right avoiding the farmyard. Follow the path straight on over the field and into the woods of Knebworth Park (the path is waymarked straight on through the trees). The path then bends right at the bottom of a slope and leads on to another high stile. Once over this, follow a narrow concrete edged path along a fence to the left. Through the trees can be seen glimpses of the lake and Chinese bridge.

Carry on along the fence to the left, to a detour through a gate to the left to get a better view of the lake and its waterside fishing cottage (an early 17th century cottage orné remodelled in the 19th century). Retrace the route back through the gate and up the concrete drive ahead towards Knebworth House through the avenue of ancient and curiously misshapen limes. (Take a break here to explore the house if open. The Barns restaurant is to the right of the house.)

At the drive crossing, bear left over the grass towards a wicket gate in the churchyard fence. North-east of the church lies the Mausoleum, all but concealed by a knot of trees. Have a look at the church in passing, then leave the churchyard by the lych gate, and follow the drive ahead past the cricket pavilion and a white gatehouse on the left onto the road. Turn right along the road, right again at the next junction and follow the road back to the Lytton Arms, where the walk began.

Historical Notes

Graffridge Wood: Part of the Knebworth estate but managed in conjunction with the Forestry Commission, it contains tumuli (probably Bronze Age), one of which lies to the right of the path near the beginning of the wood.

Knebworth House: The house is open daily from 12 noon to 5 pm from the end of May to mid-September. For other opening times and events telephone the Estate Office Tel: Stevenage (0438) 812661. The footpaths are always open to walkers.

The Lytton family have lived at Knebworth House since 1492. Sir Robert Lytton began the house in early Tudor times, building it round a large quadrangle. It remained essentially unaltered until Elizabeth Bulwer Lytton pulled down three sides and covered the remaining red brick with stucco in a renovation programme beginning in 1811. Her novelist and statesman son, Edward, then modernised it in Victorian Gothic style, embellishing it with gargoyles and battlements, and capping the towers with copper domes. The east front still looks typically Tudor despite its 19th century additions. The famous Banqueting Hall contains a great Jacobean oak screen, and a minstrels' gallery dating from about 1610. The other walls were panelled in the classical manner fifty years later. Here plays were performed in Edward Bulwer Lytton's day, one of which was attended by his friend Charles Dickens in 1850. Churchill set up his easel here in more recent times. Further renovations were made by Sir Edwin Lutyens, a Lytton son-in-law. The first Earl, another Robert Lytton, was Viceroy of India, and his son was acting Viceroy and Governor of

Bengal. These days of the raj are commemorated in a special exhibition.

The Barns: The Knebworth Barns, now housing a licensed restaurant and function room, date from the 17th and 18th centuries and were moved to their present position in 1971–2 from elsewhere on the estate.

The Gardens: The present gardens, somewhat changed from 1731 when an estate map shows orchards, a bowling green and a kitchen garden near the house, were designed by Lutyens and are famous for their pleached lime avenues. There is a pretty herb garden planted to a design by Gertrude Jekyll. Some earlier Victorian features are now being restored.

The Monument: Near the western boundary of the park, this obelisk carries an inscription by Edward Bulwer Lytton in memory of his mother. The two were not the best of friends and the Monument was not erected until 1866, some 23 years after her death.

The Church: The village church of the Virgin Mary and St Thomas of Canterbury at Old Knebworth, just inside the park, contains the Lytton chapel rebuilt in 1705 which houses some fine family monuments and Tudor brasses. The nave and chancel date from 1120. Don't miss the fulsome epitaph and bust to Judith Strode, 1662. There are various tombs designed by Lutyens in the churchyard.

Mausoleum: Built in 1817, the Grecian Mausoleum contains the remains of Elizabeth Bulwer Lytton, a strong character, who quarrelled with the rector of the day and would not set foot in the church. Lady Constance Lytton, a leader of the Suffragettes, who died in 1923, was cremated and her casket placed here.

The Lytton Arms and village street: The present pub was built in 1887 to replace little old Inn Cottage tacked onto its side. On either side of the pub along Park Lane are interesting houses and cottages dating from the 16th and 17th centuries, and the fine 18th century Manor House.

Twin lodges near the War Memorial commemorate Queen Victoria's Jubilee. Elizabeth Bulwer Lytton erected the almshouses next to the pub in 1836, and Lutyens designed various dwellings in this road (for example Mulberry Tree Cottage in 1910). He also designed handsome St Martin's Church (near the station) in 1914, and the nearby golf clubhouse in 1908.

St Paul's Walden and Whitwell

Introduction: Three large country houses, their surrounding parks and farmland, romantic ruins, the clear bubbling waters of the river Mimram, and the interesting old village of Whitwell all add up to a very varied walk which contains most of the typical features of the Hertfordshire countryside. The walk may become muddy and overgrown in places. As this is prime shooting territory, it is recommended that dogs stay on their leads. The woods here abound in deer, and the walker will be unlucky not to come upon at least one little group.

Distance: Just under 8 miles. It will take about $3\frac{1}{2}$ hours at a leisurely pace. Map – OS Landranger 166 Luton, Hertford (GR 193224).

Refreshments: The *Royal Oak* on the B656 Hitchin-Welwyn road, the *Eagle and Child*, the *Maiden's Head* and the *Bull* all in Whitwell High Street. The *Strathmore Arms* a short walk from the church in St Paul's Walden. All serve food.

How to get there: Turn right off the B656 (Hitchin to Codicote) road just after the Royal Oak pub, onto the B651 signposted to Whitwell. After two miles, take a right turn just before the Strathmore Arms pub in the hamlet of St Paul's Walden. This leads to All Saint's Church where parking is available.

The walk: Turn right out of the church and go through the gate in the churchyard wall. Set into the wall here is a Victorian letter box. Cross the road and walk down the path opposite. To the right across a meadow dotted with mature trees is the woodland garden of St Paul's Walden

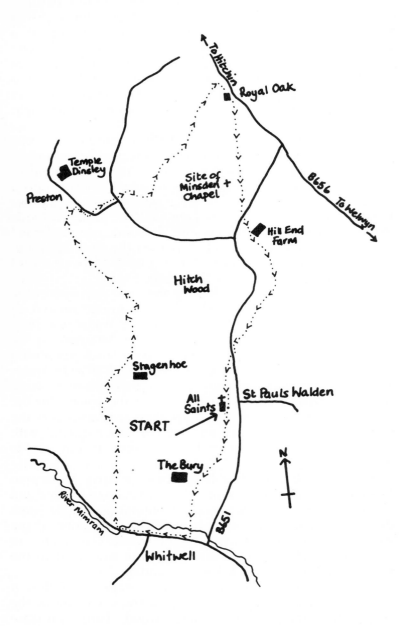

Bury. Almost hidden in trees, the octagonal brick pavilion with its pointed roof is known as the Organ House (1735) and stands at the end of a lime avenue. Further on a white statue of Venus and Adonis lurks eerily at the end of another allée. Keep straight on until the drive becomes metalled just by Gothic Garden House which backs onto a former walled vegetable garden. The main driveway approaches from the left. At a grass triangle, turn right up the drive.

Ignore the first kissing gate in the iron fence on the left, and continue on to where the drive swings right to lead to the forecourt of St Paul's Walden Bury (no public right of way). Here a second kissing gate on the left leads into a meadow. Follow the line of trees on the left to another kissing gate, and through and on into the valley towards Whitwell. Cross the wooden stile. Beyond, over a second stile, is a small concrete bridge crossing the river Mimram. Across the field is another stile which leads through a yard and onto the main street of Whitwell.

Turn right along the High Street past an interesting variety of old houses and pubs, and continue on out of the other end of the village towards the watercress beds at Nine Wells, extending along the river Mimram on the right. Just beyond, turn right up a broad track signposted to Preston, and punctuated by occasional mature trees. The path continues through another field where a large wood on the left curves fairly close to the track. On the right the imposing facade of Stagenhoe appears across the fields. Here there is still an echo of old parkland with majestic trees dotted around in the now mainly arable fields.

The footpath goes downhill, crosses a drive leading to Stagenhoe, and carries on uphill (footpath sign on tree and arrow markers) towards a wood. Continue ahead for some distance walking along a path just inside the edge of the wood carrying on past arrow markers and eventually out into a field. The footpath now skirts the woodland to the left leading to a red brick keeper's cottage.

Turn left onto the track past the cottage and follow it downhill. Turn right past a clump of trees and follow the track round uphill towards a large wood. Turn right once more round the edge of the wood which lies to the left.

Watch carefully for an iron wicket gate about a hundred yards along the wood edge, rather hidden amongst leaves and branches. Go through this gate and carry on along the path through the wood with conifers to the left and mixed hardwood to the right. Just past the firs carry straight on through the edge of the wood along a path with a hedgerow and trees to the left and a field to the right. Continue along this sometimes overgrown track; the path soon bears right and then widens out and eventually bears right to meet a roadway.

Follow the road ahead away from the white gates of Prestonhill Farm on the left, past a cottage also on the left to an intersection at a grass triangle. Here, on the outskirts of Preston, turn right past a white cottage (monogrammed at the eaves). At the next T junction, by the gates of Princess Helena College (formerly a house called Temple Dinsley), turn right along the road passing the college buildings and barns across the fields on the left, and cottages and a stud farm on the right.

Turn left at another T junction and cross the road. A little way on to the right is a footpath signposted to Little Almshoe. The narrow path continues along the fence of a pumping station and comes out into a field at a stile. Go ahead along the field edge then bear left past a spinney on the right. After the spinney cross the stile and turn left. The track continues down along the edge of an arable field past the interesting old farmhouse of Poynder's End. Continue straight on through a series of fields offering wide views over to Hitchin on the left and Stevenage on the right. The ruins of Minsden Chapel over the fields to the right provide a punctuation mark.

On reaching the B656 (Hitchin to Welwyn) road, turn right and walk in front of the Royal Oak. Just behind the far end of the pub, a signposted bridleway with a hedge then a ditch on the left sweeps leftish up the hill towards Minsden Chapel, whose ruins rise up from a tangle of brambles and nettles. The track continues on in front of the chapel following a spinney and a hedgerow on the right down towards the B651 (Whitwell) road. Cross the road. Slightly to the right along the road a signposted bridleway slants to the left up a steep bank with the road dropping away on the right hand side (the land just here is a Nature Reserve of the Herts and Middlesex Trust).

On reaching a cross track, turn left uphill past Bridleways and Hillend Farm. The path is then waymarked by two mossy boulders on the right. Cross the stile and continue straight up the hill passing another stile and keeping the hedge on the right. As the track bears right, cross over the stile between two hedges and wind down a path enclosed on either side by hedges dotted with ancient trees, allowing glimpses of small undulating fields on either side.

Cross a tiny lane, go over a stile and walk straight across an arable field with a big wood in view on the right. If the crop here makes the path invisible, skirt round the field to the right, in either case making for a wood ahead with a stile at the right hand corner, just by a stand of conifers. Having negotiated the stile, keep the woods on the left and cross through the middle of a clearing into woodland on the far side. Continue through sparse woodland along a well-defined path and out onto the road. Turn left past the gates of Stagenhoe; the antlered deer on the gateposts are a reminder of the live ones to be seen in the woods round here.

After about 50 yards turn right through the hedge (signposted but not easy to see). Cross a large field bearing leftish and follow a path marked by a ragged line of trees towards a red-brick house visible ahead. Continue along a hedge, then a fence, then once past the house, turn left down the roadway (the White House on the left is the former vicarage) and on to All Saints' Church, St Paul's Walden via the other churchyard gate.

Historical Notes

St Paul's Walden Bury: The north wing of the Bury dates from 1767 and is attributed to James Paine, while the main section of the house was built in 1887. The gracious house, with its imposing Adam-style front, is famous for being the childhood home of the Queen Mother. Equally famous in gardening circles is the formal woodland garden, the framework of which has changed little since it was laid out by Edward Gilbert in the 18th century. Geoffrey Jellicoe carried out restorations in the 1950s. The garden contains a lake, ponds, temples and statues and is open to the public on certain days each year under the National Gardens Scheme.

Whitwell: The interesting old houses in the main street retain echoes of the activities of past centuries (mill, bakehouse, tannery, brewery, abattoir, forge and straw plaiting school). Look out, too, for the Old Village Hall, a timber framed white cottage on the right of the High Street near the Bull. Whitwell watercress, still in production, was sold in London at the turn of the century, and was first produced here as far back as the 18th century.

Stagenhoe: Now a Sue Ryder Home, this 18th century mansion was formerly the seat of the eccentric Earl of Caithness. The estate also once belonged to the Earls of Derby. It was burnt down in 1737 and rebuilt three years later. Sir Arthur Sullivan lived here in the late 19th century while composing the music of the *Mikado*.

Temple Dinsley: Site of a preceptory founded in 1147, and formerly linked with the Knights Templar, this estate passed to a Benedict Ithell who built the present house in 1714. It was later remodelled by Lutyens in 1908, and eventually became a school (Princess Helena College) in 1935.

Minsden Chapel: A former chapel of ease for Hitchin, this spot was beloved by local historian Reginald Hine, who committed suicide and was buried here. It is likely that the chapel marks the site of a deserted medieval village.

All Saints' Church, St Paul's Walden: This church's 12th century origin has been largely disguised by later alterations, especially those carried out in the chancel in the early 18th century by Edward Gilbert, an ancestor of the present Royal Family who bought the St Paul's Walden Bury estate. His memorial stone is in the chapel floor. A wall tablet commemorates the baptism in 1900 of the Queen Mother in the 15th century font. The Tudor (or Hoo chapel) was built about 1579 by the important Hoo family of Hoo Manor, one of the largest estates in the parish.

WALK SEVEN

(repeat)

Hexton and Lilley Hoo

Introduction: In the north-west of the county a finger of Hertfordshire sticks up into the underbelly of Bedfordshire. Prehistoric Icknield Way cuts across this landscape, set between outcrops of the Chiltern hills, bringing with it layers of history which go back thousands of years. This walk climbs the hill near one of these early signs of civilisation, the earthworks of Iron Age Ravensburgh Castle. The walk then crosses the Icknield Way, and comes out onto the wooded tableland of Lilley Hoo, before dropping back downhill into the ancient settlement of Hexton, in its delightful setting on the edge of the Barton Hills.

Distance: The route is nearly 6 miles. Time taken is about 2½ hours. There is a SHORT CUT for those wishing to do only part of the walk. Map – OS Landranger 166 Luton, Hertford (GR 104105).

Refreshments: Pub food is available at *The Raven* at the beginning and end of the walk.

How to get there: In the centre of Hitchin follow signposts to the A505 (Luton) road. While still in the town, branch off right at a mini roundabout along the B655 signposted to Barton-le-Clay. Follow this undulating road past turns to Pirton and Pegsdon. Take the next right turn into the main street of Hexton and park near the Raven pub on the left-hand side.

The walk: Some of this walk forms part of a Circular Walk Route and is mostly signed and waymarked. Turn right out of the Raven, and walk down the main street of Hexton past the gates and high wall of Hexton Manor on the left. On the main road (B655) is the village pump erected in 1846 by Caroline de Latour of Hexton Manor. Cross the

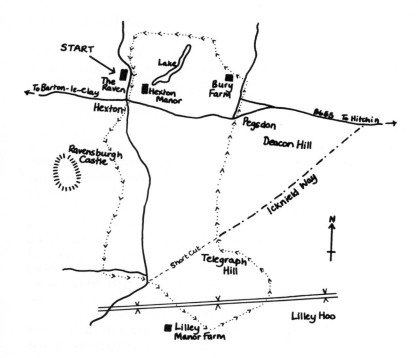

main road here and walk a little way up the road ahead (signposted to Lilley). On the right is a broad track barred by a metal gate. Duck under this and walk up the track towards woods with a wide green ride cutting through the middle. Ignore the farm road which turns right and bear left up the ride. Pause at the top to look back at the lovely view over Hexton. The track comes out into a big field with woodland to the right. Keep on the track between the field and the wood. On the far side of the wood are the banks and ditches of Ravensburgh Castle (no public access), its outlines hidden under enveloping trees. At the end of the wood, go through the hedgerow and turn right. Carry on along the edge of the wood for a short distance, then turn left along the nearest hedgerow which bisects two fields. Keep the hedgerow on the right. Over the brow of the hill can be seen a line of trees which mark a little road ahead. In a clump of trees on the right are the roofs of ancient Mortgrove Farm, for centuries part of the Hexton Manor estate. At the road turn left and admire the views over Ravensburgh Castle on the left.

Walk along the road some distance to the T junction and then turn right. At the next bend, turn left onto a short section of the Icknield Way. (Treasures Grove Picnic Area.)

(For those wishing to take the SHORT CUT, continue on along the Icknield Way until the Nature Reserve board mentioned later on is reached.)

For the longer walk, just after the entrance gate turn right off the Way along a well-defined track with a hedge on the right towards some farm buildings. Go under some power lines. Just past these, the farm track branches off to the right. Ignore this and carry on ahead instead past a wood on the right to a T junction. Turn left and follow the track downhill curving round to the right. Follow the track and the next hedgerow downhill and at a wooden signpost take the left hand route (permissive route) which leads again downhill through fields at first, then up past a wood on the right towards the tableland of Lilley Hoo. Go under the power lines again, turning left at the top at another wooden signpost. Carry on with a mixed hedgerow on the left. From this vantage point there are lovely views over the surrounding countryside. The track curves to the right, then left, still following the hedgerow. Pass two more wooden signposts keeping on the same track, then the route leaves the hedgerow and passes through the middle of fields along a wide path bearing slightly to the left towards a small knot of trees. The path goes to the right of this bumpy wooded patch and winds its way downhill through the interesting flowery banks of Telegraph Hill Nature Reserve.

At the junction of the tracks turn left to the wooden Nature Reserve board.

(The shorter route comes in here and rejoins the main walk.) Turn right, then immediately left through trees (having crossed the Icknield Way again), along another well-defined path with a wire-fenced field on the left and a copse on the right. The track continues towards a stand of conifers, through a gap in a wooden fence to a field. A right hand track goes uphill, but the walk goes straight on down a broad track with woodland on the left. The field rises quite steeply on the right towards Noon Hill and then Deacon

Hill. The broad track carries on for quite some distance downhill, and eventually comes out onto the B655.

Turn right here and walk along the verge for a little way, then cross the road to the half-timbered lodge of Hexton Manor. Follow the old road down to the outskirts of Pegsdon. Turn left at the T junction by the village sign and walk down the road. Carry straight on at the grassy triangle at the next road junction past an attractive red brick house on the left. Continue down the road signposted to Shillington past a telephone and a letter box on the left. Take the next left turn down the road through Bury Farm buildings. To the right is a good view of the half circle of hills surrounding Hexton.

Carry on along the road between cottages; the metalled road turns into a wide track with a big field on the right and a hedge and wood on the left. At the corner of a copse turn left at a three pronged bridleway sign and follow the track down towards a hedge of conifers. Soon the track passes the site of an old mill near a stream and a cottage with a pretty water garden. The track becomes metalled again with open fields on the right and trees on the left. Through a gap there is a glimpse of Hexton Manor all but hidden by woods and parkland trees. Go past the sewage treatment works on the left up to a junction where a private road goes off to the right. Go left here bending back towards the houses of Hexton, and finally back to the Raven.

Historical Notes

Hexton: Evidence of settlement at Hexton, with its favoured position just off the Icknield Way, near the hillfort of Ravensburgh Castle, goes back long before Domesday Book. When it was compiled in 1087, however, there were about 35 households in Hexton. In 1030, the Lord of the Manor was Sexi, a Dane; the manor then passed in 1031 to the Abbot of St Albans and remained under the Abbey until the Reformation. The appearance of the present village with its Edwardian estate houses is due to George Hodgson who bought the estate in 1900 and rebuilt virtually the whole village. The old Plough Inn was pulled down and the present Raven Inn built in 1913 to match the cottages. In 1914 the landlord was Wilfred Harkness who grew roses here, a business which expanded into the famous firm of Harkness Roses now based at Hitchin. The eight hundred year old church is on the main B655 road.

Hexton Manor: The present house was built in 1770 and replaced the former manor house the Burystead, bought in the 17th century by the Taverner family, the first owners actually to live in Hexton all their lives. Francis Taverner wrote the *History and Antiquities of Hexton*. The house enjoyed a tremendous period of renovation and expansion from 1815 under the ownership of Caroline de Latour (died 1869) who had been brought up at Hexton. She also laid out the park and gardens and carried out many projects in the village.

Ravensburgh Castle: The best preserved of the remaining Iron Age hill forts in the county, Ravensburgh Castle is striking for its very commanding position, somewhat disguised now by thick tree growth. On a spur of the Barton Hills about five hundred feet above sea level and just off the Icknield Way, it is oval in shape and covers 22 acres with a 50 ft ditch and an 18 ft high bank.

Icknield Way: The Icknield Way is arguably the oldest pathway in Britain, a prehistoric track along the ridge of the Chilterns connecting Wiltshire with East Anglia. Neolithic man, the Romans, the Saxons and the Vikings all used it. In places it was a series of roughly parallel tracks often forged through wooded land by herdsmen. The name is linked to the Iceni tribe, and there is a wealth of earthworks and other ancient sites along its path.

Ashwell

Introduction: Right up in the northern reaches of the county, Ashwell and its surrounding countryside are well worth exploring. Its situation near the important route of Icknield Way with clear springs bubbling below a sheltering hillside meant that at the time of Domesday, Ashwell was one of the wealthiest and most important market towns in Hertfordshire. The surrounding countryside is quite different from the rest of Hertfordshire. Huge sweeping fields under immense skies rise up to the south and west giving spectacular views; below on the plain and nearer the village, the fields become more intimate, edged with hedges and trees to shelter stock. The walk is designed to encompass the best features of the village and its countryside. From every point on the route can be seen the watchful spire of Ashwell church, dominating the scene for miles around.

Distance: 4¼ miles. Time taken about 2 hours. A SHORT CUT can be taken. Map – OS Landranger 153 Bedford, Huntingdon (GR 266398).

Refreshments: The *Bushel and Strike* and the *Rose and Crown* (both do good food and are on the route of the walk). The *Three Tuns* (food and accommodation) is a short detour from the walk.

How to get there: Leave the A1(M) from London just north of Baldock at a turn off signposted to Shefford (A507). Do not take the A507 but go round the roundabout and take the exit signposted to Baldock. Shortly after this turn left to Newnham and Ashwell. Continue along this twisting road through Newnham and down into Ashwell. Just after the VG Stores and Christy's Corner on the left, turn left, then immediately right, then left again into Mill Street. Park along here near the church.

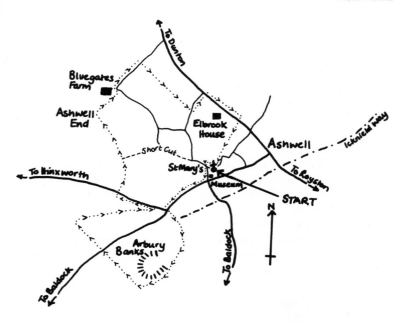

The walk: Keeping the Church of St Mary the Virgin on the left and the Bushel and Strike on the right, walk up Mill Street past the unusual double lych gate, and the cottages adjoining Swan House (the Angel Inn in 1609) on the left, and the 17th century building housing Crump's the butcher on the right. Cross the road to the Museum and turn right past the village's own cottage garden on the left and the white row of cottages (formerly the workhouse) over the green on the right. Bear left round the corner of the garden, then turn right opposite the 16th century Rose and Crown. Continue along the High Street pausing to admire Bear House on the left and 17th century Digswell Manor with a reminder of its malthouse at the rear on the right.

Walk past Bacon's Yard on the right and later on Wilson's Lane going off to the left. Notice particularly 15th century Dixies Farmhouse next to its former rectangular farmyard bounded by weatherboarded and slate roofed barns. Further on is Farrow's Farm with listed barns in its farmyard and again on the right down a drive early 16th century Westbury Farm where John Bunyan is reputed to have preached in a barn. Enclosure came late to Ashwell which accounts for the many former farms and farmyards which line the village street. Next on the right is the gateway leading to the Village Hall, once a malting of Page's Brewery with the old brewery office just inside the wall. Opposite is the Chantry House, probably the oldest house in the village.

Carry on past the left turn to Back Street past a grassy bank on the left. At the end of this, opposite the junction with the Hinxworth Road, take the rutted lane which leads uphill (Partridge Hill). Carry straight on up this, ignoring a track leading to the left (part of Ashwell Street, one of the routes of the Icknield Way), past a red-brick house built into a bank and later a terrace of white cottages on the right. Just beyond the cottages, well hidden in the hedge, is a sign saying 'Arbury Banks Ancient Monument'. This is the true line of the footpath, but the farmer prefers walkers to carry on uphill a little further to where he leaves an obvious path through the crops at right angles to the main path, leading right towards the scrubby bushes and fence of the circle of Arbury Banks ahead.

At the bushes bear left round Arbury Banks to the other side of the semi-circle, to a baulk which veers left away from Arbury Banks. Follow the track below this keeping the baulk on the left, until a short way along a right hand track near a second lower baulk and a new wood branches off at right angles across a field. Go along this over the brow of the hill and onto the Newnham to Ashwell Road. Cross this and carry on up the track opposite. This is not a right of way but the owner allows access for the time being. Walk straight on up track towards a hedge. Go through the hedge and turn right downhill. Below is spread out the Ashwell plain from Hinxworth on the left over to the villages of Bedfordshire in the distance.

Carry on downhill passing the back gardens of houses on the main road. When the path meets the road to Hinxworth turn left and walk along the road for about 150 yards. By a bungalow a right turn (signposted to Ashwell End) takes the walker along a green lane edged with a variety of trees and shrubs. Halfway along here a short cut leads back to the village.

(For the SHORT CUT, turn right off the track along a waymarked path leading past a little piece of hedgerow then along a division between two fields. Follow the field edge round to the left then turn right again down a rather scrappy hedgerow on the right and a small field on the left with a boundary hedge lined with poplars. At the time of writing all this area was a soft fruit farm. Make for a willow ahead by a stream. Turn left here keeping the stream on the right and head towards a gap in the hedge barred by three poles. Cross into the next field and walk towards a white cottage. Before reaching the cottage turn right through a gateway onto a lane at a corner. Go ahead up the lane, do not turn left, passing two pleasant houses and a left turn. Carry straight on to a fork by 18th century thatched Chain Cottage. Take the left hand fork which soon emerges onto Mill Street and the start of the walk.)

To continue the main walk, carry on along the green lane until it meets a tiny road at a bend. Carry straight on up the road (do not turn left) and continue round a right hand bend past farm buildings. At another junction of lanes carry straight on ignoring the right turn back to Ashwell. The road bends left to meet a bridge carrying the road over the stream at Bluegates Farmhouse. Turn right here away from Bluegates and follow the road up towards a group of white pantiled buildings. Just before the garden boundary here, there is a signposted right turn over a stile and across the middle of a grassy field. Make for a fence over the field in which is a second stile (footboard missing) marked by a pole. Cross this and head across the next field skirting Whitehead's Wood to the right to reach a third stile onto the road.

Turn left up the lane and right again at the next T junction by a grassy triangle. Go along the fringe of Elbrook Wood on the right, and a short way beyond the drive to Elbrook House is a wooden kissing gate (signposted to Ashwell). Go through this, along the edge of a strip of woodland on the right to another kissing gate. Go through this onto a lane. Bear right up the lane and over the stream. This is the river Rhee, a tributary of the river Cam which runs through Cambridge, and its source is just a little further upstream at the Springs. The stream runs under the renovated mill on the left (one of three mentioned in the Domesday Book) over a wheel taken from the old Fordham's Brewery over the road. The splendid Maltings on the road and the old stables further back are all that remain of the brewery buildings. The drive to Ashwell Bury is on the right with its Victorian stables just over the road. Carry on up Mill Street past 16th century estate cottages and Merchant Taylor's on the right back to the start of the walk.

Historical Notes

The Church of St Mary the Virgin: Building began in the early part of the 14th century, probab'y incorporating some materials from an earlier edifice. The chancel was completed in 1368. Ashwell church is famous for its graffiti including an important one of old St Paul's Cathedral, and two haunting inscriptions, one of 1350 referring to the Black Death which hit Ashwell particularly badly, and a later one of 1361 commemorating a dreadful storm. The church tower is one of the highest in Hertfordshire at 176 feet; its leaded spire is a typical Hertfordshire spike.

Ashwell Museum: The Museum is housed in the early Tudor Town House, and the building was once used to record and collect all the tithes due to the Abbot of Westminster. It opened as a museum in 1930 to house an ever-growing collection of exhibits collected by two local boys. The collection has continued to grow and is now a unique record of local and village life from earliest times to the present day. It is open on Sunday afternoons or by appointment.

Chantry House: Chantry means an endowed chapel for the singing of mass, but the religious connections of this attractive 15th century thatched building are rather obscure. There is an ecclesiastical looking 15th century stone window at the west end, but some say this was added later. In 1547, the Chantry House was 'in the hands of John Smarte, clerk, a man of godlie conversason', but in the 19th century it fell from grace to become a public house called The British Queen. The landlady was called the Queen of Sheba.

Arbury Banks: This hill fort probably dates from the Iron Age but there is some evidence to show that it is Bronze Age. Like Ravensburgh Castle, it was built near the route of the Icknield Way and was probably used for protection of animals as well as defence.

Bluegates Farm: An extended and modernised 16th century house, once two cottages, Bluegates is said to have been built from the timbers of a house across the stream where Henry VIII's doctor Thomas Bill once lived. There are the remains of a moat here, one of several in the parish. For a short while, the house was a pub, the Tumble Down Dick, for catering to the coprolite diggers. Coprolite was fossilised bird dung collected and ground up to use as fertiliser during the late 19th and early 20th centuries.

Ashwell Bury: This early 19th century house was altered by Sir Edwin Lutyens in 1922–6. It was used as a convalescent hospital during the First World War. The gardens were originally designed by Gertrude Jekyll.

The Springs: The Springs, source of the river Rhee which flows into the river Cam, are the main reason for Ashwell's existence and give Ashwell its name: a well by an ash tree. Descendants of that ash tree stand in the Springs basin today. The Springs have been designated a Site of Special Scientific Interest mainly because of the existence in the clear, pure water of a rare flatworm (*Crenobia alpina*), in existence since the Ice Age.

Merchant Taylor's School House: Founded in 1681 with money left by Henry Colbron (who lived at Westbury Farm), with extra classrooms added in 1849 and 1876, this building remained a school well into the 20th century when it was taken over by Hertfordshire County Council. It was built of Ashwell bricks with a stone tablet over the door, commemorating Colbron's gift. In 1947, the school became a Further Education Centre and Library and in 1968 Ashwell Field Studies Centre was added.

Newsells and Cokenach

Introduction: Lying between the villages of Barley and Barkway in north-east Hertfordshire are the two neighbouring estates of Newsells and Cokenach. The countryside here is fairly high and rolling offering good views over fields and woods to surrounding villages. The houses and cottages of Newsells have now been sold to individuals but the estate retains a beautiful and timeless quality. The fields round the great house at Cokenach are larger and flatter than the intimate undulating fields of Newsells, but there is still plenty of woodland to make the walk varied and interesting. Short detours can be made to explore the pretty villages of Barley and Barkway. The land is chalky downland and the lovely wild flowers of that habitat flourish on verges and waste ground.

Distance: About 7 miles. Time taken approximately 3 hours. There are two possible SHORT CUTS. Map – OS Landranger 154 Cambridge (GR 385360).

Refreshments: The *Chaise and Pair* and the *Talley Ho* in Barkway, the *Chequers* and the *Fox and Hounds* in Barley all serve food.

How to get there: Barkway is down a lane off the A10 just south of Royston. Go through the village of Reed following a small road, eventually turning right at a T junction to reach Barkway at a junction with the B1368. Turn left for a short way here and park in the village hall car park.

The walk: Leave the car park and cross the road going a little way left to a public bridleway signpost pointing to Newsells. Turn right along the narrow path here which first goes through trees and then bears right along the edge of a field on the left. A radio mast is in clear view over the

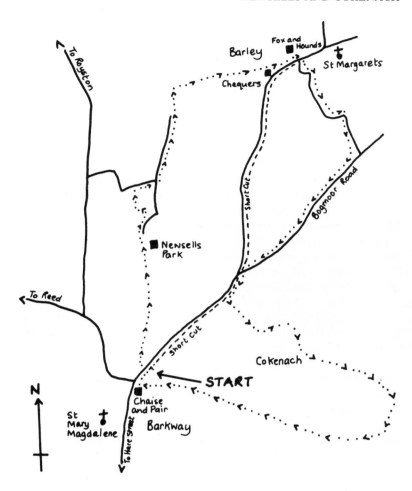

field. Follow the rather overgrown track with a fence on the right. The path comes to a crossroads of ways near some well-fenced fields. Carry straight on between fences. There is an obelisk in the parkland on the right and the ground slopes down to red-brick colonnaded Newsells Park house. The track goes on downhill between a fence on the right and a hedge on the left. Pass a small Gothic thatched cottage of the early 1800s on the right and go through a gate onto a lane. Turn right along this, but almost immediately there is a blue and yellow plastic arrow on a post pointing to the left down a broad track. Go through the gates here and follow

61

a track overhung with trees. The red-brick walls of an old kitchen garden rise over on the right. Follow the curves of the track round to the left and to the right by a 'Private' sign and carry on through more open fenced land. Pass a thatched cottage on the right and come out onto a lane.

Turn right passing another beautiful thatched cottage high up on the left. The lane ends in a T junction by a boulder inscribed with the names of the Newsells men who lost their lives in the First World War. Turn left here and walk along a shady lane. Pass Fox Cottage on the left and carry straight on along a broad, open track with the land rising quite steeply on the left. At a T junction of tracks turn right over a bridge and continue on along another broad track which becomes metalled as it reaches the outlying dwellings of Barley. Carry straight on at a junction of lanes, passing the Chequers pub on the right to reach the B1368. For a SHORT CUT turn right here and follow this sometimes busy road for a mile or so back to Barkway and the car park.

For the full walk, turn left along the main road (London Road) walking along the pavement. The Fox and Hounds pub is a little further on along this road but the walk turns off before the pub. Ignore the footpath signed to the left but shortly after this cross the road to turn right down Smith's End Lane which weaves through barns and cottages passing Noble's Cottage dated around 1370 on the left. Ignore the footpaths signed to right and left and carry on along the lane, passing a fascinating array of houses and cottages of varying ages, including Smith's End Farm where you can buy dried flowers. Follow the curves of the lane past the cricket ground on the left and more pretty cottages until the lane goes out into open countryside. There are wide views on the left over Barley to the windmill on the road to Great Chishill. At a T junction of lanes turn right at the signpost to Barkway, ignoring the signposted footpath ahead. The lane, called Bogmoor Road, describes what the terrain must have been like in bygone days. Now it is a dry open road with high banks which are host to a marvellous selection of chalkland wild flowers. Follow the road for nearly a mile enjoying the views down into Newsells Park. Pass cottages on the right and reach the B1368. Turn left for a short distance signposted to Barkway and Braughing. Here is another opportunity for a SHORT CUT by continuing along the main road.

To follow the rest of the walk, turn left up the driveway to Cokenach (public bridleway signpost on the verge opposite). Carry on up the drive through an avenue of trees. There is a cricket ground over on the right. The drive curves sharply to the left and divides, the right hand branch leading to Cokenach house. Take the left branch and follow it round. Ignore a concrete track going off to the left and keep bearing round to the right. There are views of the impressive front of Cokenach house and its moat through the shrubbery on the right. At an array of farm buildings keep to the left and carry on past a row of huge green-painted feed stores (or silos) on the left. Then turn left along a broad track through trees which leads away from the farm buildings.

The stony track becomes part concreted and continues on through open fields towards woods ahead. A row of trees borders the track on the left. When these end go ahead for a short distance to where the track bends to the left. There is a wooden footpath signpost on the right with one arm broken. Turn right here. The line of the footpath veers slightly away from the ditch on the right towards another footpath signpost across the field, but if there is no track left through crops walk along the edge of the ditch. At the signpost or near a crossing of ditches turn right and go ahead across a bridge over the ditch, carrying on ahead along another ditch on the left towards a stand of trees. The path should pass between these mature trees on the left and some newly planted ones, but the undergrowth can make this difficult in places. At the end of this little block of woodland keep on ahead along the edge of the ditch on the left and a field on the right. As you arrive at more woodland on the right there is a wooden footbridge. Cross this, then turn left over another bridge, turning immediately right to carry on again ahead, this time with the ditch on the right bordering a wood. At another block of woodland ahead carry straight on along a broad green track. There is now a ditch on the left. Ignore a bridge crossing this into the wood and carry on along the edge of Earl's Wood (bluebells in spring) on the left with views of Cokenach house and its interesting stable block over the field on the right.

At the end of the wood there is a crossing of tracks.

Continue ahead along a metalled path towards a house. Turn right before reaching this along a mixed shrub hedge, then shortly left by a plastic arrow marker post pointing through the hedge. Go ahead along the edge of a garden and continue along a track with a barbed wire fence and then a field on the left and open land dotted with trees on the right. At the end of the field avoid a wide green track which comes in from the right and go ahead by a yellow arrowed post through a rough area of trees and scrub following the well-used narrow track to the left then shortly right again to eventually come through a gap onto the recreation ground at a yellow arrow post. Skirt round the recreation ground towards the left-hand corner. Here another footpath signpost points ahead down a mud track between fences past the car park of the Chaise and Pair pub on the left to come out onto the road (the B1368) at the war memorial. Turn right to reach the Village Hall car park again. To make a detour along the interesting main street of Barkway with the Tally Ho pub at the other end turn left at the war memorial.

Historical Notes

Barkway: The long High Street is made up of an interesting selection of attractive houses of varying periods including several coaching inns, which point to Barkway's one-time importance as a staging post. Look out for a splendid milestone, one of several set up on the route to Cambridge in 1725 by a Master of Trinity Hall. It bears the coat of arms of the college together with those of one of the two Elizabethan fellows whose bequest to the college provided the funds to carry out the work. Thatched Berg Cottage of 1687 belongs to the National Trust. The church of St Mary Magdalene just off the High Street past the old horsepond has a 13th century chancel and contains many memorials dedicated to past owners of the Newsells and Cokenach estates. One of 1743 to Admiral Sir John Jennings by the famous sculptor Rysbrack was sent back here because it was too big for its designated space in Westminster Abbey.

Newsells Park and hamlet: Newsells was a significant settlement in Domesday times with 44 tenants and, like

Cokenach, may well have become depopulated because the land was given over to sheep. The Queen Anne manor house was burnt down in the last war and replaced with a neo-Georgian red-brick mansion. The splendid old stables still stand and nearby is an attractive 17th century dower house. The estate cottages are a pretty mixture of thatch and plaster or mellow brick.

Barley: Most people remember Barley because of the distinctive inn sign spanning the village street of hounds chasing a fox. The pub attached to it is 17th century. Also of interest are the timber-framed 17th century lock-up and the early Tudor Town House with its original roof timbering. St Margaret's church was restored by Butterfield in 1872 and has a Norman tower and an arcaded 14th century south aisle. The splendid pulpit dates from 1626. Two rectors of Barley became Archbishops of Canterbury.

Cokenach: In contrast to the small fields, dells and spinneys of Newsells, the parkland of Cokenach is vast and flat, broken up with large chunks of woodland. The large house dates from 1716, with additions in 1833 and 1925, and is moated. The nearby farmyard consists of lovely stables dating from the mid 19th century and an interesting collection of barns and farm buildings. There was a village here but the population moved on when the land was used for sheep farming by the Prior of Royston. In 1901 the writer Rider Haggard stayed here with owner Alexander Crossman.

Buntingford, Aspenden and Throcking

Introduction: This triangular walk meanders between three fascinating small churches each one of which is a short detour off the main walk. Along the way the walker has a taste of an old turnpike town and its associated river, two sites of deserted villages, and the rolling farmland in between. The footpaths cross several arable fields but in each case clear tracks through the crops have been left by helpful farmers.

Distance: The route is about 6 miles and will take about 2½–3 hours at a leisurely pace with detours but without extra exploration. Map – OS Landranger 166 Luton, Hertford (GR 361298).

Refreshments: The *Red Lion* (a detour to the left down the main street of Aspenden), the *Fox and Duck*, Church Street, Buntingford, the *Jolly Sailors* by the bridge in Buntingford (bar snacks and restaurant), the *Chequers*, High Street, Buntingford (light snacks).

How to get there: Buntingford is on the A10 (London to Cambridge) road. Coming from the direction of London, avoid the new A10 bypass and at a roundabout just outside Buntingford follow the signs into the town. Turn left in the centre onto the A507 (Baldock) road. Take the first right signposted to the car park.

The walk: From the car park, walk to the left down the footpath beside the Gateway supermarket, cross the old A10, turn right along it for a short distance, then left down Church Street past some pretty cottages and the Fox and Duck pub at the bottom. Cross the river Rib

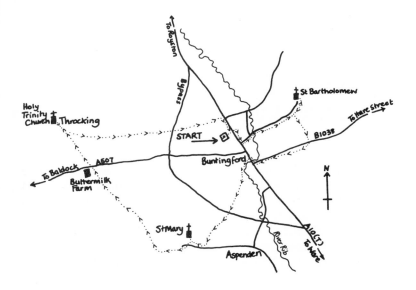

either by the humped bridge, near the now restored early 18th century red-brick lock-up, or for more excitement, turn left a little way to the causeway by a ford almost opposite pargetted Bridewell House (built in 1491 as a house of correction, then the Waggon and Horses Inn before 1700). Over the river a road called The Causeway leads uphill with the old mellow wall of Little Court on the left, past a school further up on the right, becoming a hedged lane further up. The lane bears left at the top of the hill to the half-ruined church of St Bartholomew at Layston with its nostalgic graveyard through a gate across the lane.

Pause to enjoy the atmosphere of this romantic spot, full of birdsong and wild flowers, then return along the lane past a footpath signpost on the left, to where a broad grassy path by a horse chestnut tree leads left across a field to a distant road. Here there is a good view down into Buntingford punctuated by the green spire of the Roman Catholic church of Sir Richard of Chichester (1915), while the white chimney ahead is the only indication of the vast Sainsbury depot on the edge of the town. The red-roofed timber framed building over the fields to the left is Alswick Hall, site of another deserted village.

On reaching the road, turn right and down past houses and allotments to the old A10 just by the Jolly Sailors pub. Cross and turn right over the river Rib to an oddly shaped red-brick building with a milestone of about 1742 against the east wall, St Peter's Church. Further down the High Street from the church can be seen the 18th century pump under its pumphouse built in 1897 to commemorate Queen Victoria's Diamond Jubilee. Behind the church is the beautifully proportioned facade of the Seth Ward Almshouses.

Carry on round the church to the left, then right down a roadway by the river bordered by attractive cottages and pretty riverside gardens. The road turns into a path. Avoid the continuation of the path to the right between houses, and go ahead along a track which eventually comes out into a new housing estate. Follow the signposted route past a sports centre, turn right up an estate road and then shortly left down Knight's Close. Go to the end of the close, then along a path between houses which comes out at a field boundary. Continue on diagonally across the next field towards a fence and stile giving onto the Buntingford bypass. Cross with care, negotiate the stile on the far side and make for the hedgerow and an old oak tree with a huge trunk almost split in two. Turn right here along the edge of a field keeping the hedge on the right, and go ahead onto a path. This in turn leads to a broad track which passes through a pretty woodland glade down into Aspenden. The track emerges onto the main village street between Regency Aspenden Lodge on the left and Bell House (built in 1714 for squire Ralph Freman and formerly a school) on the right. Turn left here for about a hundred yards if you wish to visit the pub.

Otherwise, turn right along the road bordered by a deep ditch with an assortment of bridges leading to different houses. Make a small detour at the end of the lane to St Mary's Church on the right. Next to the church, gates lead to Aspenden Hall and Tudor Stud.

Return to the corner and take the wide track on the right signposted to Throcking. The track bears to the right away from the trees and then turns left to go to early 18th century Tannis Hall. Ignore this and follow the public footpath straight on up a grassy path by a new copse. After about three quarters of a mile the copse gives way to a fence and a hedgerow. The path turns sharply to the left and then to the right again towards a group of buildings along the road which includes 16th century timbered Buttermilk Hall under its old red tiled roof. Go through an iron gate, and then straight down between gardens towards wooden gates. The gates lead onto the road between modern houses.

Turn left along the verge, then cross the road and take the first right turn (signposted to Throcking) along a quiet little lane towards Holy Trinity Church almost hidden in trees in the distance. The church and neighbouring farm are now the only indications of a village deserted centuries ago. Having made a detour to the right at the road junction to go and look at the church, return to this point and strike off along a broad track to the left signposted to Buntingford. This leafy avenue of mature oaks leads downhill through gently undulating countryside with woodland on the left. When the trees end, follow the line of the track over the brow of the hill through the middle of an arable field towards a small gap in the middle of trees and a hedgerow ahead. A backward glance shows the church at Throcking dominating the peaceful fields. Pass through the hedge between two wooden posts and carry on up a division between two fields (a small baulk) towards the corner of a copse. Ahead is the footbridge over the bypass leading the eye up towards Layston church on the hill ahead. After the bridge the track passes between two schools to a road. Cross the road and follow the path straight on past allotments. Turn right at the old A10 past the Chequers pub. Notice the street scene here, a delightful mixture of cottages and houses of all ages. Before turning right up the alley by the Gateway supermarket, glance up at the 16th century clock and clock tower arching over the pathway.

Historical Notes

St Bartholomew's Church, Layston: This was once the centre of the Anglo-Saxon village of Layston which became deserted as its population gradually moved downhill towards Roman Ermine Street and the river, the main lines of communication. The early 13th century chancel is still in use as a chapel for the nearby cemetery.

Buntingford: Roman Ermine Street once forded the river Rib which passes through the middle of this dignified market town. This route increased in importance over the years (in 1663 Parliament authorised the first turnpike road in England through Buntingford) and the town became a useful stop on the stagecoach route. Later on a rail link added to the town's accessibility.

St Peter's Church, Buntingford: Originally a 13th century chapel of ease for Layston, the present building is dated 1615 (see inscription on the east gable). This mellow brick building in the shape of a Greek Cross became the parish church of Buntingford when the church at Layston was finally abandoned. It was restored in 1899 when the north porch was added, and contains a brass dedicated to its benefactor Dr Strange.

Seth Ward Almshouses: Beautifully built in brick with mullioned windows and a pediment and inscription tablet over the central door, these almshouses were founded in 1684 by Bishop Seth Ward, a mathematician and astronomer, who became finally President of the Royal Society.

St Mary's Church, Aspenden: This picturesque medieval church dominates its prettily planted churchyard from a small hillock. The chancel lancets date back to the 13th century. The south-east chapel of 1622 contains an early Tudor monument to Robert Clifford who betrayed his friends in the Perkin Warbeck conspiracy in the late 15th century. The church was restored in 1873 by Blomfield who added the steep red tiled roof and the gabled dormers.

Aspenden Hall: This stately classical house was built in 1856 for Sir Henry Lushington to replace the earlier Jacobean house. It used to house a school run by the

Reverend Matthew Preston which the historian Lord Macaulay attended for a while. It was gutted in 1963 for farm use.

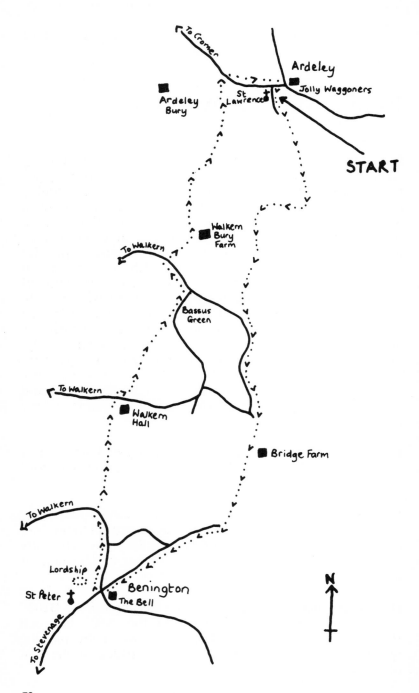

START

To Cromer

Ardeley

Jolly Waggoners

Ardeley
Bury

St Lawrence

Walkem
Bury
Farm

To Walkern

Bassus
Green

To Walkern

Walkem
Hall

Bridge Farm

To Walkern

Lordship

St Peter

Benington

The Bell

To Stevenage

N

WALK ELEVEN

Benington and Ardeley

Introduction: The green lanes and bridleways linking Ardeley with Benington lead the walker between two very different but equally interesting villages. Ardeley is more of a hamlet with the special attraction of a picturesque green, edged with Arts and Crafts type thatched cottages and incorporating a thatched village hall and an interesting communal pump house. Opposite is the village pond and the lovely 13th century church of St Lawrence. The pretty and varied dwellings of Benington date back much further as here was the site of an important castle and, even earlier, the residence of kings of Mercia. Most of the castle at the Lordship is now demolished and in its place are an interesting folly, an imposing early 18th century house and an exquisite garden open to the public. Both villages are within easy reach of the town of Stevenage but feel very rural and remote because they are approached by a network of tiny lanes.

Distance: About 6½ miles. Time taken 2½–3 hours at a leisurely pace. Map – OS Landranger 166 Luton, Hertford (GR 308270).

Refreshments: The *Bell* in Benington serves real ales. Pub lunches are available every day except Sunday and evening meals on Thursday, Friday and Saturday. The *Jolly Waggoner's* in Ardeley does excellent bar and restaurant meals.

How to get there: Ardeley is down a turning off the B1037 which runs between Stevenage and the A507 between Baldock and Buntingford. There are two layby parking spaces outside the church, and more parking at the end of School Lane.

The walk: Turn down School Lane which is just past the church. Keeping the houses on the right, go ahead down a bridleway. Although rather muddy and scruffy to start with, this turns into a broad green lane passing through unspoilt rolling farmland with plenty of trees and woods all around. Avoid the two field paths which veer off the main bridleway fairly early on. A large farm track then goes off on the right but continue along the main path which becomes more overgrown and overhung by trees on either side. The track comes out into more open countryside with a field leading to a wood on the right. Continue on. A sign warns 'Caution Clay Shooting – Keep Out'. The main track veers to the left.

This walk takes another green lane branching off to the right here. It looks very overgrown to start with but the undergrowth soon clears and the ancient route is tunnelled over with coppiced trees, mainly hazel. Continue along this lane for about a quarter of a mile, then look very carefully on the left where there are some larger trees for a small track which turns left into a field. Follow this along the edge of the field with a wood on the right towards a hedgerow with a gate in it. Go through the gate. There is a public footpath through the middle of the field ahead but it may not be marked through the crop. With your back to the gate look over the arable field ahead towards woods and take a slightly left diagonal track through the crop, passing a dip with a clump of scrub in it on the left, making for a corner which sticks out a little in the middle of the woodland ahead. At the fenced-off corner of woodland walk ahead alongside the wood on the right towards more woodland. Turn right through a gateway along a broad track through this fringe of woodland and follow the track round to the left, walking along the edge of a field on the right and woodland on the left. Over the fields on the right is a view of the imposing stable block of Walkern Hall.

Turn left along a quiet leafy lane passing a red brick house on the left. At a road junction bear left (No Through Road sign). Turn right along a broad stony track signposted to Bridges Farm (red arrow marker on post). Where a hedgerow comes in on the left and right, abandon the stony track which curves left to the farm and go ahead following the line of a hedge on the left along a broad track by the edge of a field on the right (red arrow marker on post on the right). Follow the curves of this field-edge path, which soon has a ditch on the left, towards woodland. Continue along the edge of the mixed woodland and when it ends continue to follow the track round the edge of the field. At one point a blue arrowed marker points to the left but continue on. The track goes through woodland along a very muddy stretch churned up by horses. Eventually the track comes out at a gravelled crossing of tracks marked by another post with blue arrows. Continue ahead along metalled Duck Lane into Benington, emerging onto the main road by a large duckpond on the right. The entrance to Benington Lordship is to the right of the green ahead and the church is further on down the road. A short detour to the left past lovely cottages brings you to the Bell pub.

To continue the walk turn right along the pavement and walk up Walkern Road passing Old School Green on the right. Further on past some bungalows on the right a well-signposted footpath takes you to the right along a concrete driveway lined with poplar trees leading to Walkern Hall. Go through a metal gate to the left of the driveway to the hall and continue on along a stony track with a good view of the Regency hall to the right. Go through another metal gate onto the road, ignoring a Circular Walk sign which points to the left and turn right for a short distance along the road passing a farm duckpond on the left and the stable block of the hall on the right.

Turn left just past the farmhouse down a concrete track (footpath signpost in hedge) passing farm buildings on the left and go ahead along a broad stony track by a band of trees on the right which offers views over the rolling countryside. The path goes down into a dip, over a stream and up the other side towards the lovely thatched roofs of Bassus Green ahead. At the road turn left to reach the crossroads on the green itself.

Turn left here and walk along the road until a sign (Public Byway) points up a broad stony track on the right. A notice indicates that this is to Walkern Bury Farm only. Turn left at a junction of tracks before reaching the farm down a track which is signposted 'Private Drive No Vehicles'. The farmhouse is sited near a Norman bailey with a deep ditch and bank. The track goes downhill passing between hedges and trees and giving good views over Walkern on the left. Avoid cross tracks and go gently uphill to a T junction of tracks. Bear right here passing a public path signpost and go up a broad grassy track between crops. The path narrows and bends to the left to go through a strip of woodland, passing a blue arrow marker post on the left. It emerges into a field with Ardeley church punctuating the distant view ahead. Follow the track down the edge of the field with a strip of woodland on the left. There is a good view of turreted Ardeley Bury through a gap in the hedge on the left. The path meanders uphill between trees and scrub with a disused pit on the right and comes out onto a concrete farm track passing a bungalow on the left to reach the road. Over the road is a calvary set into the bank. Turn right along the road and follow it back into the village of Ardeley noting the pleasant green opposite the church and pond. There is a lovely pub called the Jolly Waggoners a little further on.

Historical Notes

Ardeley: The model village green with thatched cottages, a thatched village hall and an attractive central pumphouse, all designed in 1917 by F. C. Eden, were the brainchild of the then landowner John Carter of Ardeley Bury and Dr Eck the vicar. The inscription on one of the houses, 'Auspicium melioris aevis' ('A sign of better times') must have brought a ray of hope during the dark days of war. There is a war memorial and garden of remembrance in front of the church.

Church of St Lawrence: The church has a lovely early English chancel and a fine piscina and lancet windows in the north aisle. Twelve beautifully carved angels with outstretched wings hold up the old roof. There are interesting monuments and brasses of 1515, 1599 and 1885. F. C. Eden (responsible for the green) also restored the church, adding a rood in 1928. The nearby vicarage is Jacobean.

Ardeley Bury: Glimpses of this house through the trees show a basically Tudor building restored in the Gothic style in about 1820 with a romantic turret and battlements. Sir Henry Chauncy, author of *The Historical Antiquities of Hertfordshire*, lived here in the 17th century. His brother emigrated to America and eventually became the first President of Harvard University. The manor was owned by the Chauncy family from 1572 to 1803.

Benington Lordship: The beautiful gardens of the Lordship slope steeply down to ancient fishponds fed by the river Beane. The present red brick house was built in about 1700 on the site of a farmhouse owned by the Caesar family who lived at nearby Benington Park. The present appearance of the house and folly date from Victorian times when the property was given a neo-Norman look when the gatehouse, summerhouse and curtain wall were added. The site was especially important in Saxon times. It was said to be the residence of kings of Mercia and in 850 a council was held here by Bertulf when reports came that the Danes had invaded and captured Canterbury and London. Later the manor was granted by William the Conqueror to Peter de Valognes whose son built a square stone keep, the ruins of which are still apparent today along with an outer bailey, moat and inner bailey.

Church of St Peter: The church nestles beneath the ruins of the old castle halfway up a steep slope. John de Benstede, Keeper to Edward I of the Great Seal and of the Wardrobe, owned the manor in 1285 and built the church. His coat of arms can be seen on the tower and in the 14th century porch, which also has a carving of St Michael slaying a dragon. Other Benstedes, commemorated by tombs and memorials in the church, added their contributions, in particular Petronilla, wife of Sir John, who built the chapel and the beautiful arches separating it from the chancel in 1330. The Caesar family, descended from an Italian doctor who ministered to Queen Mary and Queen Elizabeth I, owned the manor from 1614 until 1741 and are also represented in the church.

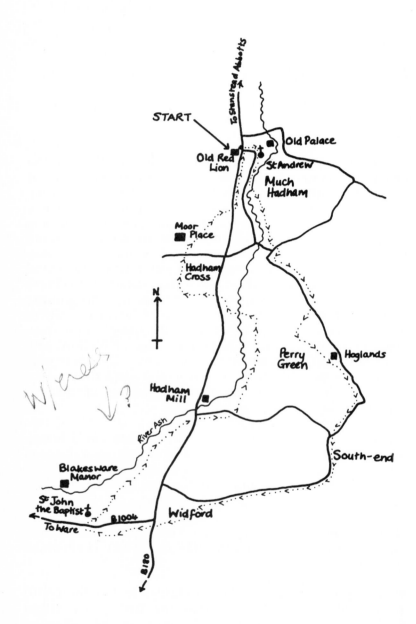

Repeat! 9/96

Much Hadham and Widford

(Good winters walk)

Introduction: This walk introduces the rambler to the beautiful countryside in the east of the county towards its border with Essex. It begins in the large, handsome village of Much Hadham, where the long main street is a wonderful lesson in history and architecture encompassing an extraordinary variety of Elizabethan cottages, and grand houses of the 18th and 19th centuries. Leaving the river Ash which meanders through woods and water meadows behind the houses of Much Hadham, the walker strikes out to Perry Green and takes a footpath passing through the grounds of Henry Moore's home at the time of his death, where gigantic pieces of sculpture enhance the beautiful grounds. After Perry Green comes the pretty village of Widford with its associations with essayist Charles Lamb. The route goes down from the church to the river Ash, and then passes through the fields and woods of the river valley back towards Much Hadham.

Distance: 7 miles approximately. Time taken 2½–3 hours. This walk can be wet and muddy after rain so wellington boots are recommended. There are two SHORT CUTS if required. Map – OS Landranger 167 Chelmsford (GR 428197).

Refreshments: _Hoops Inn_, Perry Green, the _Green Man_, and the _Bell_, Widford and the _Bull Inn_, Much Hadham all serve food.

How to get there: Leave the Cambridge to London (A10) road north of Ware, and follow the Bishop's Stortford (A120) road. Not long after the turn, in the village of Standon, by the Bell pub, take a right turn signposted to

Much Hadham. Follow this winding road for about 3 miles until a T junction is reached. Turn right into Much Hadham and park fairly near the beginning of the village opposite the Old Red Lion.

The walk: Turn left off the High Street and walk down the Causeway towards St Andrew's Church. To the left of the church, behind a wall, is a glimpse of the Old Palace and to the right of the church, again behind a wall, the 17th century Old Rectory. Bear right round the corner past some pargetted cottages and follow this pretty lane, running alongside the river, hidden in woods on the left, to another bend by a house called Two Bridges.

Cross the stile here into a meadow and walk left along a fence and over a foot-bridge. Walk through the next meadow keeping left to the end of a straggly hedgerow where an iron kissing gate leads over a drive to a stile to the right of a five barred gate. Go over the stile and straight ahead through this meadow towards some cottages in the distance. The river is now to the right. Cross a stile, bear a little to the right by some scrappy trees which lead to yet another stile by a gate and onto a lane. Turn left up the lane, and at a T junction turn right. The road bears round to the left. Follow it uphill through steeply rising woodlands on either side, past two dwellings on the left, until more open country is reached further on.

At the top of the hill is the village of Perry Green. Walk past cottages on the left and take a footpath through the field on the right, just before a road junction by the unusual stone chapel of St Thomas. The track is clear through the field, and leads towards a large oak ahead. Here a track goes off right to Much Hadham (which can be used as a SHORT CUT) but the walk continues on past another oak, to a third (rather blasted) oak where there is a T junction of tracks. Turn left here towards some farm buildings. Follow a broad green ride past the farmyard on the left and a fenced-off field on the right. At the bottom of the field turn left onto a gravelled track over a stile by a gate. This track goes through the grounds of the Henry Moore Foundation and allows glimpses of various pieces of sculpture set in the lovely gardens.

At the road, turn right down a lane past the Hoops Inn on the left. Further down the lane, at a junction where a letter box stands in the middle of a green triangle, take the right fork past a pond, houses and a school. Turn left at the next road junction by a 'No Through Road' sign. This lane is a causeway going through fascinating wetlands of ditches and ponds outside cottages and farms (look out for several fine weathervanes, especially the one belonging to Turtle Farm).

The road eventually bears round to the right becoming a gravelled lane. After an unusual thatched cottage on the left, the lane becomes a muddy track lined with an avenue of oaks with open fields on either side. Make for a white cottage visible ahead. A path branches off to the right back to Hadham Mill, but the walk carries straight on along the track past cottages on the right. Just past a thatched building on the right bounded by a flint wall, turn left over a stile (signposted) to a gate and a stile the other side of a small meadow. Cross the second stile and continue along a narrow path between a field on the left and a hedgerow on the right. On reaching a derelict brick building on the left, turn right along a hedgerow, through some wooden gates, over a track leading into a farmyard, and onto the road past a large house in the village of Widford. For refreshment turn right down the road to the Green Man or carry on to the Bell.

To continue the walk, turn left along the road to the Bell pub on the other side of the road. Turn right down Bell Lane, just before the pub, then left along the main road past a cricket pitch with a thatched pavilion and Ashview Nursing Home on the left. The road turns into Abbot's Lane which bears slightly to the right and offers lovely views over the valley towards Blakesware Manor on the hillside opposite. The Church of St John the Baptist is outside the village on the right standing high on the hillside. The path goes through the churchyard to the left of the church passing a handsome archway in an old brick wall.

Go over the stile, down a slope with rough steep steps, into the valley of the river Ash. Make for a muddy, cow-trampled gap in a fence and go towards the river. Turn right along the river bank, keeping the river on the left. Pass a footbridge on the left but do not cross

WATERCRESS ! (see p. 96)

it. Instead carry on alongside some bushes to a stile near sewage works on the left. Cross the stile. A second stile ahead leads back to Widford, but take the left-hand path along the river between two wire fences, across another small field towards a tiny road. Cross this and walk down a concrete track leading to waterworks. At the gates bear left into the field and carry on ahead along a fenced path. The field gives onto a bridleway between a field on the right and a fence and hedgerow on the left. A sign names this path as Toto's Way. Eventually this path comes out onto the road near lovely old Hadham Mill.

The road opposite is signposted to Perry Green and Green Tye. Cross and walk a short way up the road. Turn left at a gatehouse into a large old quarry (a Herts County Council Depot and tip). Bear left past the weighbridge and head for a black single bar gate and posts which mark the beginning of the bridleway to Hadham Cross. (Do not go to the right where a track goes uphill.) The cinder track is good here and passes through mixed woodland by the river on the left. Further on past a larger stretch of water seen through the trees on the left the track eventually comes to a more open clearing with a field on the right. Look out here for a track going to the left, which passes over a little bridge towards a brick sub-station. Continue along this fenced track and walk up a hedgerow past the sub-station on the left. At the main road turn right and walk along the footpath to a garage. For a SHORT CUT continue along the main road here back to the Old Red Lion. For the main walk, cross the road here and go up a lane called Station Road. The station is now demolished; the last train ran in 1965. At the junction at the top, take a right hand fork past some council houses. The road curves round to the right, but just before this, take a left hand track towards a house, and carry on along it past the backs of houses to a stile at the end of the lane. Cross the stile and turn left through the middle of a field towards a road.

Cross the road, go up steps on the far side and through a kissing gate by a cottage on the left, into the grounds of Moor Place. Cross a farm road and walk diagonally right across a small field to a stile in the fence leading down from farm cottages ahead. Walk diagonally right again across a field and over another stile. Look left over the field to the splendid facade of Moor Place. Go towards a line of trees and a stile in the corner of the field by a conifer hedge and tennis courts, and thence onto the drive. Turn right down the drive, through the gate to the left of the main gates, and left onto Much Hadham High Street. The walker is now offered a feast of fascinating buildings of all ages and shapes on both sides of the High Street. Look out particularly for Plummers (formerly the Post Office) with its jettied first floor, the Forge Museum owned by the Herts Buildings Preservation Trust, the Hall of 1725 behind a mellow old garden wall and pleached limes (until recently the home of the son of poet Walter de la Mare), the Bull Inn (a tavern at least as far back as 1727), Campden Cottage (once the headquarters of the Hertfordshire Society), the Old Rose and Crown whose brick front hides a much older timber structure, and Northleys the Georgian chequered brick house on the left, next to the Old Red Lion.

Historical Notes

St Andrew's Church, Much Hadham: Set in a beautiful churchyard which runs down to the river, St Andrew's Church is a mixture of later styles which have largely masked its 12th century origin. There are 14th century arches with highly decorative capitals. There is plenty of rich 15th century work including the chancel, nave roof, screen and pulpit, and a wealth of finely carved details. The church contains several interesting brasses, some good stained glass and a pair of heads by Henry Moore flanking the tower doorway. A sign over the main door reads 'This is the Gate to Heaven'.

The Old Palace: A will of AD 946 of a Saxon queen left lands in Much Hadham to the Bishops of London, who continued to own and use the property for 900 years. The present building is 16th century and timber framed, faced in brick in the late 17th century. A floor was inserted in the original Great Hall, and a Jacobean staircase and panelling added. The Bishops of London used it as a summer residence until 1746; it later became a school, a lunatic asylum, and finally a private residence broken up into several units.

Perry Green and Hoglands: Chiefly famous for being the home and workplace of Henry Moore, who died in recent years. He lived at Hoglands, now called Danetree Cottage, which is administered by the Henry Moore Foundation (please contact the Foundation for details of Open Days and events).

Widford and Blakesware: Essayist Charles Lamb held the countryside around Widford and Blakesware in high esteem. He was born in 1775 (died 1834) and spent a lot of time in the area as his grandmother, Mary Field, was housekeeper at Blakesware, and is buried in the churchyard at Widford.

Church of St John the Baptist, Widford: Built of flint and stone from Barnack in Nottinghamshire, this little church dates back to the 12th century (see Norman mouldings above the south wall), though the nave dates from mid 13th century with the chancel a little later, and the tower is 14th century. The church contains interesting murals, one dating from 1299.

Moor Place: The present house is an elegant five bay brick house of 1775 built on the site of a 16th century house owned by a William Moore. The stable block is of the early 18th century, and garden walls of the earlier house still survive. The coat of arms of James Gordon dated 1779 is over the main doorway.

The Old Red Lion: This interesting building dates back to 1483. In 1577 it was known as the Angel, and the name was changed to the Red Lion in 1720. It closed as a public house in 1971. Renovations in 1925 brought to light Tudor panelling and a hidden staircase and passageway, and more gruesomely, the skeleton of a 17 year old girl.

Hertingfordbury and Panshanger

Introduction: Near the county town of Hertford is the village of Hertingfordbury, set in a peaceful hollow, surrounded by fields sloping down to the river Mimram, and fringed to the north by the beech woods of Panshanger. The A414 bypass has diverted the noisy and destructive traffic from the village, allowing it to breathe and relax once more. The line of the old railway passes through Hertingfordbury and the collection of Greens. The walk follows part of the line and then turns up through Birch Green onto the Panshanger estate. A special Station at Cole Green was built to serve the big house at Panshanger, now sadly demolished. Remnants of Panshanger's park, landscaped by Humphrey Repton, still survive, and the walk passes through some beautiful parts of the estate.

Distance: 7 miles. Time taken about 3 hours, at a leisurely pace. Map - OS Landranger 166 Luton, Hertford (GR 309118).

Refreshments: The *White Horse Hotel* (food and accommodation) and the *Prince of Wales* (bar food), both in Hertingfordbury.

How to get there: Turn off the A1(M) at Stevenage South. Follow the signs to Hertford (A602). On the outskirts of Hertford at a mini roundabout near the station, turn right onto the Welwyn (B1000) road. At a roundabout, turn left to Hertingfordbury, crossing the A414 at another roundabout just at the approach to the village. Follow the village street until just past the White Horse Hotel on the opposite side of the road, a left-hand fork (St Mary's Lane) leads up past the church. Carry on out of the village to a

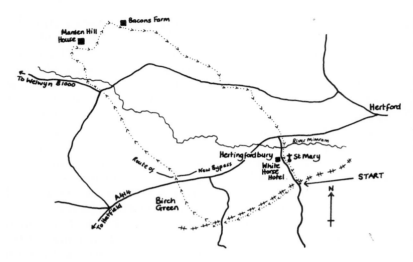

small railway bridge. Turn left just after this to park in a lay-by next to the Cole Green Way.

The walk: This walk is waymarked most of the way. Climb steps up a bank by a notice explaining a permissive right of way, turn left and walk over the bridge along the line of a disused railway. This is part of the Cole Green Way. Walk straight on until the way ahead is blocked by undergrowth. Take one of the two choices of steps up the right-hand bank, cross a small road, and descend again to the railway line through a fence (sign says Birch Green 1 km) down more steps (again two choices). A little way along this section of the track, take a right-hand path down the bank and over a stile into a field. Go ahead along the fence on the right towards some houses ahead. Cross a stile and make for a path lined with privet hedges which goes under an archway through the houses, and out onto the road at Birch Green. Go down the road ahead and bear right still passing through houses on either side of the road. Cross the road and follow the wide verge or green towards the main road. On the right-hand side of the side road is the old village school with a green painted Victorian letter-box set into the wall.

Cross the main road and turn left for a short distance; then turn right down a footpath signposted to Poplar's Green, past weather-boarded cottages on the left and a pond on the right. Go into the drive of Poplar's Farm and turn left following a diagonal path across a field and new garden planting (stile in fence). Go through the hedge in the corner, then turn immediately right, back through a hedge, and walk along the track towards a footbridge over a new bypass. Once across the bridge, follow the path bearing left along the edge of woodland on the right for some distance. The path bears right, goes between fencing through a more open area of bracken, and then downhill. The beautifully treed area on the hillside ahead and to the right is the location of the demolished Panshanger mansion.

Go down into a clearing over a stile at the bottom of the slope, straight across a field towards a wood on the other side. Cross another stile and walk on to a rough roadway. Near this point is the famous Panshanger Oak (unfortunately on private ground). Cross the roadway on a long diagonal, leaving it to walk ahead along a broad grassy path towards Poplar's Green Lodge. Climb over the stile next to the gate here, and out onto the road. Cross and walk down the slip road to the Welwyn (B1000) road. Turn left up the main road for a few yards, then take a path on the right over a stile (signposted), which crosses a beautiful old bridge over the river Mimram. Cross a stile and then take the path which goes diagonally to the left across a field towards trees on the far side.

At the trees turn left along the field edge, then just before a big oak tree, turn right through a gap in a fence, marked with a yellow arrow. Bear rightish and continue gently uphill along the edge of a field with a hedgerow and trees, then a fence on the right. At the corner of the field, turn right across a stile into another field. Go ahead by trees and a fence on the left. Eventually the path passes a ha-ha on the left in front of Marden Hill House.

After the ha-ha, at the end of a metal fence, bear left, over a stile, and over the drive to Marden Hill House. Follow the track straight ahead past Mereden Cottage with its wonderful barn on the left, down the drive and out onto a small road (to Tewin). Cross the road to a field ahead and walk down the edge keeping woodlands to the right. Continue on to a stile but do not cross it. Instead turn right down the edge of a field. A wire fence with a farmhouse beyond stretches along on the left. Turn left at the end of the fence into another field past farm buildings. Bear left here, then right, onto a good gravelly path. Go some way down this lane which is hedged on both sides, then across a little road and onto a bridleway signposted to Hertford Road straight ahead. Walk along this towards some woods. Follow the bridleway through the edge of Sele Broom Woods. Then walk down the next field, keeping a hedge on the left. At a junction of tracks bear right and out onto the B1000.

Cross the road and turn left, continuing along it nearly as far as the houses on the outskirts of Hertford. Go through a kissing gate on the right by a public footpath sign and cross a field towards a wood. Through another kissing gate into the wood, the track follows on downhill and then goes along the edge of a field on the right and through a clearing. At the end of the field, the path goes to the right towards more woods. At another notice the public footpath bends to the left, and, a little way along it, a permissive route veers to the right, down into a picnic site and out onto the road near a roundabout on the A414. Bear right to the roundabout. Cross the dual carriageway, then turn right and left down into Hertingfordbury.

Carry on along the main street past an old yellow brick mill on one side of the road and the Moat House (with its unusual outbuilding) on the other. The White Horse Hotel on the right now belongs to Trust House Forte. A short distance further on up the right hand fork of the road is the Prince of Wales pub. To return to the start of the walk, bear left near the White Horse, up St Mary's Lane past St Mary's Church on the left and the drive to Hertingfordbury Park (now a school and nursing home) with its little Dutch gabled gatehouse. The lane continues on past the cricket pitch on the left back to the bridge of the disused railway.

Historical Notes

The Cole Green Way: This Hertfordshire County Council route for walkers, cyclists and riders runs from the outskirts of Hertford almost to Welwyn, ending up on the A414 just beyond Cole Green. It follows the line of a disused railway, a branch line from Welwyn to Hertford which was opened in 1858 and finally closed completely in 1966.

The last passenger train ran in 1951. An interesting variety of plants and trees can be seen along its length ranging from the opportunist saplings and scrub on the banks to the low-growing flowers and plants colonising the track and its edges. Birds enjoy the undisturbed cover on the banks.

Birch Green: Birch Green was originally a Saxon settlement formed in a clearing in the thick wooded cover where water could be obtained. There were once seven similar greens but now only five are still significant centres of population. All are in the vicinity of the old railway.

Panshanger: Panshanger was an amazing Gothic mansion, the home of the Cowper family for two centuries. The last owner, Lord Desborough, sold the estate to a gravel company in 1953 and the mansion was demolished. The grounds were landscaped in 1801 by Humphrey Repton for the fifth Earl Cowper, and remnants of this beautiful parkland still remain – the river Mimram winds its way through the grounds expanding to a lake below the site of the mansion. The Cowper family were linked by marriage to Lord Melbourne of nearby Brocket Hall (he was Prime Minister in 1834). His sister Emily married Earl Cowper but the marriage was not a success. She had two children by Lord Palmerston, who himself twice became Prime Minister, and she married him when Earl Cowper died. The first Earl Cowper (a Lord Chancellor) had a brother who was involved in an unsavoury murder trial. A monument to him (by Roubiliac) plus several other Cowper monuments are in Hertingfordbury Church.

Panshanger Oak: The famous Panshanger Oak (protected by a tree preservation order in 1953) is probably over 500 years old. Gilbert White, the 18th century naturalist, calls it 'probably the finest and most stately oak now growing in the South East of England'. In 1876 a contemporary writer described it as having passed its prime with decay setting in. In 1906, its girth measured 21ft 4in at 5ft from the ground. Today it is still kept alive by branches which have touched the ground and rooted. It grows in the former pleasure gardens of Panshanger.

Hertingfordbury: This village of pleasant 16th, 17th and 18th century houses, some with curious architectural features, is well worth exploring. The White Horse, with its Georgian facade hiding a 16th century core, has always been an important hostelry and now has been extended into a large hotel run by the Trust House Forte group. In 1086 Hertingfordbury had two mills; the present 18th century mill with its yellow brick cladding stands by the bridge at the beginning of the village.

The Church of St Mary: Though heavily restored in the 19th century, the church has several earlier features including a 13th century chancel and nave. It contains many interesting monuments, mainly to the Cowper family of Panshanger. The pulpit and lectern, the altar back and rails, and the font are all made of rose alabaster.

WALK FOURTEEN

Essendon and Little Berkhamsted

Introduction: Essendon is part of an oasis of unspoilt countryside in the south-east of Hertfordshire which is ringed all round by large conurbations with the outskirts of London just to the south. This lovely village stands high on a hill overlooking meadows and woodland and the pretty valley of the river Lea. The walk reaches the outskirts of the equally attractive village of Little Berkhamsted (not to be confused with the town of the same name in the west of the county) before passing through farmland and a very fancy golf course (complete with new ponds and terracotta statuary) to return to Essendon. The terrain is mostly woods, meadows and roughly cultivated fields – all very friendly to wildlife.

Distance: About 5 miles. Time taken 2–2½ hours at a leisurely pace. Some parts of the route can be quite muddy, rutted and overgrown. A SHORT CUT is possible but not recommended as it follows the main road. Map – OS Landranger 166 Luton, Hertford (GR 273088).

Refreshments: The *Salisbury Crest* and the *Rose and Crown* in Essendon, the *Candlestick* in Essendon West End and the *Five Horseshoes* in Little Berkhamsted all provide food.

How to get there: Essendon is on the B158 which is reached via the B1455 off the A414 between Hertford and Hatfield. Park near the church just off the main road.

The walk: From the church follow the lane which leads to West End, passing pretty houses and cottages, some adorned with the Salisbury crest, until the ancient pub of the same name is reached. Just past the pub turn left down

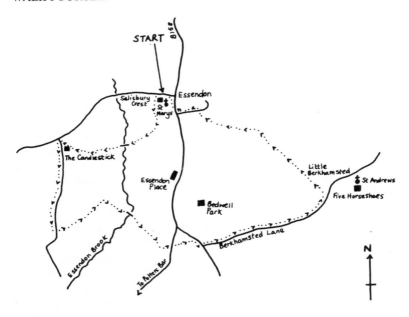

a signposted footpath (Essendon West End). Go through
a kissing gate and walk diagonally rightish through the
paddock here. Go through a gateway by a stile. Avoid
the track coming in from the left and go slightly to the
right over a stile to the left of wooden gates. Walk down
the hedgerow on the left to another stile to the left of a
wooden gate and there a wooden footpath signpost points
diagonally right over the field towards woods.

Cross a stile in the fence and turn right along the cross
track here which goes along the edge of the woods on
the left. Continue ahead through woodland along a hedge
of yews on the left. Cross a stile and keep on ahead
through more open woodland following the well-trodden
path. This goes on downhill through brambles and scrub
dotted with young trees, with lovely views over rolling
countryside, then descends steeply through more woodland.
Go through a gap in a hedgerow and carry on straight
ahead across a small meadow, ignoring a path back to
the left. Go over a bridge and straight on through a
gap in a hedge. Go ahead up the edge of a field with
a partial hedgerow on the right. At the end of the field

go through a gap in the hedge to meet a broad cross track.

Turn left for a short distance and watch carefully for a wooden signpost almost hidden in woods on the right. It indicates a bridleway with blue arrows which goes straight on and a footpath marked by yellow arrows which crosses it. Turn right along the narrow footpath through a strip of woodland. Come out into a huge rolling field with a knot of trees in the middle and turn right up a thick hedgerow on the right. Looking back you can see Essendon Place dominating the landscape. Climb a stile and follow a narrow path gently uphill through trees and scrub. Go over a stile to the right of a wooden gate and through the garden of the Candlestick pub, which is dotted with plenty of welcoming bench tables – ideal for a drink and rest.

Turn left past the pub along a pretty lane with lovely country views. There are glimpses through the trees of Essendon Place again on the far hillside on the left. The lane curves to the left passing through mixed woodland and then it climbs uphill through more open land. Another wood begins on the left and before long there is an opening into it marked by blue arrows on a post. Camfield Place (see Historical Notes below) is about a mile further on along the lane.

Turn left off the road down this bridleway – a broad, rather rutted and muddy track through mixed woodland. Follow the curve of the track, which now goes through a fringe of woodland through which fields can be seen on either side. After about ½ mile a wooden marker post on the left points the bridleway straight on with a blue arrow while a yellow arrow indicates a footpath to the right. Take this and cross a fence, coming out of the strip of woodland into a field. Turn right down the edge of the field and follow the fringe of woodland on the right, walking roughly parallel to a row of pylons on the left. The electric wires disappear into the wood just past a large oak tree, and here an unmarked opening leads to a path to the right. Follow this through rather nettley and overgrown woodland, then cross over a wooden footbridge and carry straight on. On either side of the track along most of its length are moss-covered banks with signs of old coppiced trees indicating that this route has been a well-used way for hundreds of years. Ford over a tiny side stream and at a cross track marked by the remains of metal kissing gates ignore the left hand track which leads to a bridge and carry straight on, bearing left after a short distance to cross a second bridge. Climb the steep bank on the other side and go up through the trees, then climb a stile and go up wooden steps to the road. For a SHORT CUT here turn left along the main road.

For the main walk, cross the road and take the track immediately opposite which is signposted to Berkhamsted Lane. Walk between fences with a cupressus hedge on the left for part of the way then pass alongside trees bordering a sunken lane on the left and paddocks on the right. The track comes out by a bungalow on the right. Cross the road here and walk up Berkhamsted Lane (the sign on one side of the lane is spelt Berkamstead and on the other side Berkhamsted – the council must be hedging its bets on the correct spelling). After two houses on the right the lane passes through hedged fields; on the left is a strip of woodland bordering a golf course. There are views of red brick and turretted Bedwell Park House through the trees. Continue on down and then uphill along the lane for about ¾ mile, then turn left through smart white gates by a lodge (bridleway signpost). Before doing this a detour can be made by going on a little further along the road to reach Little Berkhamsted church and the Five Horseshoes pub just down a right turn by the war memorial. Ahead can be spotted the curious red brick battlemented tower of Stratton's Folly.

Continuing the main walk, having turned left by the lodge, carry straight on down a gravelled drive past more white gates on the left and a fenced paddock, then pass a farmyard on the right and a house on the left. The track becomes more muddy and passes a large new farm barn on the right. Go through a small gate to the right of farm gates carrying a notice about dogs on leads. The track is now a wide bridleway running between fences and offering a good view of Bedwell Park on the left. The track leads downhill and passes through a wooden gate into a wood. The path narrows through the wood. Pass a white cottage on the left and go through a wooden barred gap to the left of a metal gate, and on through a former farmyard, now part of a golf complex. Follow the roadway up to the golf clubhouse (a smart conversion of an old barn) and turn right just before it (the footpath is well signposted through the golf course). Follow the slip road round, bearing left at the next corner. Carry on ahead where the golf track bears right and go through fencing by a footpath signpost. Go ahead up the path, ignoring a farm entrance on the left, and come onto a roadway. Turn left along this (School Lane), passing the village hall and the pretty Old Schoolhouse of 1853 on the right backed by a housing estate, to reach the main road (B158) running through Essendon. A short detour to the left takes you to the Rose and Crown pub, but it is not far right along the main road before you turn leftish up Church Street signposted to West End back to the church and the Salisbury Crest pub.

Historical Notes

Essendon: There are several large and important houses in the neighbourhood. Essendon Place is a white Regency house set in interestingly planted terraced grounds. It is now used as a training centre for the Electricity Board. Turreted Bedwell Park, once the home of the Whitbread brewing family, is now a country club, while Camfield Place, which was much loved by Beatrix Potter who used to stay here as a child, is the home of romantic novelist Barbara Cartland. Pretty houses and cottages near the church sport the Salisbury crest showing links with the Salisbury family of nearby Hatfield House.

St Mary's Church: The ancient building with its 15th century tower was restored in 1883. The east end of the building was destroyed by a Zeppelin in 1916 which fortunately did not damage the lovely black Wedgwood font of 1778 given by Mary Whitbread of nearby Bedwell Park. Don't miss the lovely brass monument depicting the large family of William Tooke who died in 1558. In the graveyard is the tomb of the Reverend Richard Orme who died in 1843. He was so worried about being buried alive that his tomb is above ground with a door. He was buried with a key to that door together with a bottle of wine and a loaf of bread! Also buried in the graveyard is Vice-Admiral Sir Sydney Fremantle, who was senior naval officer at Scapa Flow in

1919. On the day of the Treaty of Versailles he had taken all his ships to sea, which involved him in controversy when he missed the scuttling of the German fleet of warships.

Little Berkhamsted: Opposite the church is a pretty row of old weatherboarded cottages. Little Berkhamsted House is Georgian, while Gage House is Elizabethan. In its grounds is Stratton's Folly, a 100ft tall brick battlemented tower of 1789 with classical cornices. It was built as an observatory by a retired admiral.

St Andrew's Church: This unusual 17th century building was converted in Victorian times. It has an unusual east window by Rosenkrantz dating back to 1919. Bishop Ken, the notable clergyman and author of several famous hymns, has his initials carved on the altar made in the 1890s. He was born in the village and was made Bishop of Bath and Wells in 1685 by Charles II even though he had criticised the latter for his immoral lifestyle. Living through the Monmouth Rebellion, he was sent to the tower by King James II for speaking out against his Declaration of Indulgence. He was later deprived of his see and retired to Longleat, where he was looked after by his benefactor, Viscount Weymouth.